The Erich Fromm Reader

The Erich Fromm Reader

Erich Fromm

Readings selected and edited by
Rainer Funk

Foreword by
Joel Kovel

Humanity Books
An Imprint of Prometheus Books

59 John Glenn Drive
Amherst, New York 14228-2197

Published in German in 1985 as *Erich-Fromm-Lesebuch* by Verlags-Anstatt, Stuttgart. Introductions and compilation copyright © 1985 by Rainer Funk. © 1985 by the Estate of Erich Fromm.

Published 1999 by Humanity Books, an imprint of Prometheus Books

03 02 01 00   6 5 4 3

Library of Congress Cataloging-in-Publication Data

Fromm, Erich, 1900–1980.
    [Selections. 1998]
    The Erich Fromm reader / Erich Fromm ; readings selected and edited by Rainer Funk ; foreword by Joel Kovel.
        p.   cm.
    Originally published in English 1994.
    Includes bibliographical references (p.   ) and index.
    ISBN 1–57392–479–2 (cloth : alk. paper). — ISBN 1–57392–462–8 (paper : alk. paper)
    1. Social psychology. 2. Humanistic psychology. 3. Character. I. Funk, Rainer. II. Title.
[HM251.F77725   1998]
302—dc21   98–52762
                                                                              CIP

Printed in the United States of America on acid-free paper

Contents

Foreword to the English Edition

A generation after his death, Erich Fromm's message is more timely than ever—timely, yet also forgotten and neglected, and nowhere more so than by the psychoanalytic establishment. Occasionally articles appear in the literature belaboring psychoanalysis for its neglect of the real lives of adults and its inadequate social theory. However, it is rarely observed that there was a famous psychoanalyst named Erich Fromm who belabored psychoanalysis for the same reasons—a man who had much to say about real life and society and who, for more than thirty years, vigorously challenged Freud's vision of human existence and set forth a radical alternative. That this powerful voice should no longer come to mind when psychoanalysis defines itself is not a simple forgetting. It is, rather, an act of repression.

The ostensible reason for the schism between Fromm and Freud was the former's attack on the latter's libido theory. Fromm consistently argued that Freud exaggerated the erotic dimension, giving the sexual meanings of neurosis unwarranted primacy over all others and burdening psychoanalytic theory with a drive-defense model better suited for zoology than the study of human beings. Fromm was not, of course, unique in this. But he was an exceptionally visible and articulate critic, and perhaps the most public figure associated with psychoanalysis during the middle years of the century.

But then a remarkable thing happened: Barely twenty years after Freud's death, it appeared as if the profession started to take Fromm's advice, without recognizing the fact. Psychoanalysis began extricating itself from precisely the biologistic and mechanistic thinking against which he had inveighed. Of course, Fromm, long consigned to irrelevancy, was not heeded in any literal sense. Nevertheless, psychoanalysis found itself following the path he had set for himself. One began to hear that although in practice psychoanalysis was about meanings, it remained stuck with a theory that emphasized forces. This was exactly Fromm's point and was soon to be codified in a substantial revision of theory itself. In time, the castration and Oedipal complexes with which Freud had anchored his libido theory were downgraded from the status of master code. As they declined in explanatory value, other, less biologistic foci such as object relations, attachment, and individuation came to the fore. Mother-infant relations became of competing and, in some hands, prior importance compared to the patricentered Freudian view of human conflict and development. And the psychology of the self, with its attendant focus on narcissism, began competing with the traditional ego psychology and its drive-defense model.

All this ferment has decentered the classical Freudian position and fundamentally revised psychoanalytic thought. The reader of this collection will have no difficulty finding each of these points of revision in Erich Fromm's reflections on the human condition, articulated years—and in some cases, decades—before they found their way into the mainstream. It was Fromm who emphasized sociality, matricentricity, and the importance of healthy narcissism before the profession as a whole came to these views. And yet Fromm remains a nonperson within the world of psychoanalysis instead of being hailed as one of its most prescient visionaries. Why?

There is a rejoinder: Fromm was so ultimately disengaged from the psychoanalytic point of view as to make his critique irrelevant; he showed little interest in problems of therapeutic practice or technique. He failed to even leave a mark among the so-called neo-Freudians, unlike his contemporaries Karen Horney and Harry Stack Sullivan, who succeeded in building substantial movements within psychoanalysis. It could also be argued that Fromm exemplifies the adage about throwing the baby out with the bathwater. Too often he seems less interested in modifying the biologism and patriarchy of classical psychoanalysis than in jettisoning the Freudian discoveries altogether. As a result, one finds in Fromm little of Freud's inspired delving into the dialectics of the inner world—a dialectic whose negative pole is defined by the erotic. For Fromm, the erotic seems bracketed, or even off the map. Subsumed into relations of power or intimacy, Eros loses its place—and human subjectivity loses a dimension.

Granted, these are shortcomings. But they certainly do not account for the repression of Fromm. The above limits notwithstanding, Fromm should still be commemorated as the man who pointed the way beyond the patriarchal and biologistic assumptions of classical psychoanalysis. That he is not so recognized concerns another, more radically heretical aspect of his worldview. In distinction to both the analytic establishment and his neo-Freudian colleagues, Fromm insists on not simply a social point of view but a social view that is explicitly emancipatory. Established psychoanalysis does not mind a social dimension so long as this dimension is kept within the bounds of the normal. Psychoanalysis, after all, had no problem incorporating Heinz Hartmann's theory of ego adaptation, since the adaptation was to the prevailing set of social relations. But once the boundaries of adaptation are pushed to the transformation of those social relations and, by implication, to the transformation of the ego itself, psychoanalysis not merely loses interest but becomes actively hostile.

Since psychoanalysts tend to eschew overt political controversy, they do not become openly hostile or even debate points of view such as these. Instead they declare the views off-limits to the profession and forget those who propounded them. This, essentially, is what happened to Erich Fromm.

Fromm is often identified as a humanist within psychology and psychoanalysis, and the term is certainly accurate insofar as it corresponds to his description of himself. But there is an important qualification to be made about Fromm's humanism—and to this overworked term in general. One boundary of humanism is fairly clear: It places what is specific about human beings at the center. Contrast this to the view of the Christian right, which attacks whatever denies its fundamentalist theocentrism as secular humanism, or to Freud's biocentric instinct theory. Of this latter, Fromm writes (p. 141, below): "The central problem of man is not that of his libido; it is that of dichotomies inherent in his existence, his separateness, alienation, suffering, his fear of freedom, his wish for union, his capacity for hate and destruction, his capacity for love and union"—in short, those things that specifically belong to our existence as human beings.

All this is unexceptional, and humanistic psychologists would have little difficulty recognizing the core of their doctrine in it. There is a problem, however. The above definition is only a set of words—fine words, no doubt, but vague and without specificity or frame of reference. They were not vague to Fromm, however, though his meaning might jar with the conventional one, or even with the conventional meaning given by humanistic psychology. In the following passage from Beyond the Chains of Illusion, *Fromm gives his understanding of the unconscious (pp. 80–81, below):*

The content of the unconscious, then, is neither the good nor the evil, the rational nor the irrational; it is both; it is all that is human. The unconscious is the whole man—minus that part of him which corresponds to his society. *Consciousness represents social man, the accidental limitations set by the historical situations into which an individual is thrown. Unconsciousness represents univeral man, the whole man, rooted in the cosmos; it represents the plant in him, the animal in him, the spirit in him; it represents his past, down to the dawn of human existence, and it represents his future up to the day when man will have become fully human, and when nature will be humanized as man will be "naturalized." To become aware of one's unconscious means to get in touch with one's full humanity and to do away with barriers which society erects within each man and, consequently, between each man and his fellow man. To attain this aim fully is difficult and a rare occurrence; to approximate it is in the grasp of everybody, as it constitutes the emancipation of man from the socially conditioned alienation from himself and humankind. Nationalism and xenophobia are* the opposite poles to the humanistic experience brought about by becoming aware of one's unconscious. [Emphasis in original.]

This remarkable passage contains the rub that distinguishes Erich Fromm from the bulk of humanistic psychologists no less than from the Freudian establishment. Its message is elementary: The chains that bind our humanity are social, and there can be no personal transformation without social transformation, because "to do away with barriers which society erects" is a political project. It is not a conventionally liberal political project, however, for the progenitor of this passage is none other than Karl Marx, whose message Fromm essentially translates into depth-psychological terms. Not only the spirit but the letter of these phrases is drawn from Marx; for example, in the opening lines of the Eighteenth Brumaire of Louis Napoleon, Marx writes of the nightmare of history into which we are accidentally thrown and must transform. More significantly, we find here a transmission of Marx's 1844 Manuscripts, a document that calls for a humanized nature and a naturalized man, to be achieved precisely by the "emancipation of man from the socially conditioned alienation from himself and humankind." This is the meaning to be given to alienation in Fromm's understanding of humanism—the alienation Marx discovered in the worker under capitalism, alienation from the product of labor, from the process of labor, from "species-being" (i.e., our human nature itself), and from other workers, which is to say from other people. Perhaps the most valuable of Fromm's contributions is the attention given to alienation in social psychology, a view that demolishes the standard model of neurosis and therapy. As he shows convincingly, what ails us is not internal, "inside the head," but a whole way of being, turning the self into an object and a commodity and marketing that objectified self. Thus neurosis is a mode of participating in capitalist society and reproducing that society rather than any kind of disease or disorder (to call attention to the prevailing shibboleth of psychodiagnosis) that lies at the core of neurotic suffering. And the goal of treatment must be the complete transformation of the person rather than adjustment to the given order of things. Obviously, views of this sort do not endear one to the mental health establishment.

Marx's 1844 Manuscripts laid buried in archives throughout most of the history of Marxism. The formation of the First, Second, and Third Internationals, the whole of Lenin's life, and the ascension of Stalin all took place before they were brought to light in 1932—which, as it turns out, is the year Fromm began making his contributions to psychoanalysis. His life's work may therefore be read as a set of variations on the themes laid down by the young Marx. This would be no surprise to Fromm himself, who wrote a long and ardent introduction to an edition of the Manuscripts in which he identified the *true spirit of Marx as humanism and the true spirit of humanism as socialism. It was an identity he claimed for himself and advanced energetically by encouraging and publishing similar-minded intellectuals from both sides of the Iron Curtain.*

The early history of psychoanalysis may be read as a series of reprises of Freud's original libido theory. Those who accepted the notions of libido and instinct, as Freud defined the terms, remained within the fold. Those who refused became apostates. What distinguishes Fromm from those who denied the primacy of libido, a line beginning with Jung and Adler and not yet exhausted, is the introduction of Marx's humanism—the humanism of the 1844 Manuscripts—in place of Freudian instinct theory. This emphasis also distinguishes him from the other psychoanalytic Marxists of the time, notably Wilhelm Reich and Otto Fenichel, who chose a different path of synthesis. They held on to libido theory (in Reich's case, eventually expanding it into the concept of the orgone) and tried to integrate this with dialectical materialism (i.e., Soviet Marxism), the theoretical instrument of the Stalinist apparatus. As the disasters of this system became evident, Reich and Fenichel were forced to change. Reich turned against Soviet Marxism and created his own biocentric and cosmological system; Fenichel turned underground and developed a kind of Marxist samizdat with a small cell of like-minded analysts. Only Fromm, who had not been saddled with Stalinism, was free to develop a socialist-humanist psychoanalysis as part of what he called a democratic decentralizing socialism.

Fromm, therefore, is unique. He claimed—as he says in this collection—Jung's view of a nonspecific life energy without taking Jung's path toward mystification and political reaction. And his socialism did not degenerate, as did Adler's, into petit bourgeois reformism, nor was it crippled by an association with Stalinism. Instead, he sailed on, magnificent in his idealism and full of vision, as open to Buddhism as to Marxism. He stumbled more than once and left more questions than answers, but of all the psychoanalysts, Erich Fromm remains the most universal and the most generous of spirit. And the questions he left behind remain crucial in these troubled, tribalistic times. The final collapse of Stalinism has cleared the way for a regeneration of socialist thought and practice. The intractable crises of capitalism remain mirrored in crisis and stagnation within psychoanalysis. Fromm's humanism may not provide any blueprints for renewal, but renewal is unthinkable without its perspective.

JOEL KOVEL

Acknowledgments

"The Approach to a Psychoanalytic Social Psychology" is taken from *The Dogma of Christ and Other Essays on Religion, Psychology, and Culture*, by Erich Fromm (New York: Holt, Rinehart and Winston, 1963), 3–9. Copyright © 1955, 1958, 1963 by Erich Fromm. Reprinted by permission of Henry Holt and Company, Inc.

"Social Psychology as a Combination of Psychoanalysis and Historical Materialism" is taken from "The Method and Function of an Analytic Social Psychology," in *The Crisis of Psychoanalysis* by Erich Fromm (New York: Holt, Rinehart and Winston, 1963), 114–16, 121, 123–34. Copyright © 1955, 1958, 1963 by Erich Fromm. Reprinted by permission of Henry Holt and Company, Inc.

"The Dynamic Concept of Character" is taken from *Social Character in a Mexican Village: A Sociopsychoanalytic Study*, by Erich Fromm and Michael Maccoby (Englewood Cliffs: Prentice Hall, 1970), 8–16. Copyright © 1970 by Erich Fromm and Michael Maccoby.

"The Social Character and Its Functions" is taken from the appendix "Character and the Social Process" in *Escape from Freedom*, by Erich Fromm (New York: Ferrar and Rinehart, 1941), 277–87. Copyright © 1941, 1969 by Erich Fromm. Reprinted by permission of Henry Holt and Company, Inc.

"The Authoritarian Character" is taken from *Escape from Freedom* by Erich Fromm (New York: Ferrar and Rinehart, 1941), 163–73. Copyright © 1941, 1969 by Erich Fromm. Reprinted by permission of Henry Holt and Company, Inc.

"The Marketing Orientation" is taken from *Man for Himself*, by Erich Fromm (New York: Rinehart and Co., 1947), 67–78. Copyright © 1947, 1975 by Erich Fromm. Reprinted by permission of Henry Holt and Company, Inc.

"The Necrophilous Character" is taken from *The Anatomy of Human Destructiveness*, by Erich Fromm (New York, Holt, Rinehart and Winston, 1973), 332–33, 337–43, 350–51, 365–68. Copyright © 1973 by Erich Fromm. Reprinted by permission of Henry Holt and Company, Inc.

"The Significance of the Theory of Mother Right for Today" is taken from *The Crisis of Psychoanalysis* by Erich Fromm (New York: Holt, Rinehart and Winston, 1970), 79–83. Copyright © 1970 by Erich Fromm. Reprinted by permission of Henry Holt and Company, Inc.

"The Theory of Mother Right and Social Psychology" is taken from *The Crisis of Psychoanalysis* by Erich Fromm (New York: Holt, Rinehart and Winston, 1970), 100–109. Copyright © 1970 by Erich Fromm. Reprinted by permission of Henry Holt and Company, Inc.

"The Social Unconscious" is taken from *Beyond the Chains of Illusion*, by Erich Fromm (New York: Simon and Schuster, 1962), 88, 114–23, 125–29. Copyright © 1962 by Pocket Books, Inc., renewed by the Estate of Erich Fromm. Reprinted by permission of Pocket Books, a division of Simon and Schuster, Inc.

"The Sick Society: On the Pathology of Normalcy" is taken from *The Sane Society* by Erich Fromm (New York: Rinehart and Winston, Inc., 1955), 12–19. Copyright © 1955, 1983 by Erich Fromm. Reprinted by permission of Henry Holt and Company, Inc.

"Steps to a New Society" is taken from *The Sane Society* by Erich Fromm (New York: Rinehart and Winston, Inc., 1955) 270–74, copyright © 1955, 1983 by Erich Fromm, reprinted by permission of Henry Holt and Company, Inc.; and from *The Revolution of Hope: Toward a Humanized Technology* by Erich Fromm (New York: Harper and Row, 1968), 151–58, copyright © 1968 by Erich Fromm, reprinted by permission of the Estate of Erich Fromm.

"On the Search for the Nature of Man" is taken from *The Nature of Man* by Erich Fromm and Ramón Xirau (New York: Macmillan, 1968), 3–11. Copyright © 1969 by The Macmillan Company, reprinted by permission of Macmillan Publishing Company.

"Freedom and the Growth of the Self" is taken from *Escape from Freedom* by Erich Fromm (New York: Ferrar and Rinehart, 1941), 24–37. Copyright © 1941, 1969 by Erich Fromm. Reprinted by permission of Henry Holt and Company, Inc.

"The Art of Loving" is taken from *The Art of Loving* by Erich Fromm (New York: Harper and Row, 1956), 18–26. Copyright © 1956 by Erich Fromm. Reprinted by permission of HarperCollins Publishers.

"Self-Love, Selfishness, Selflessness" is taken from *Man for Himself* by Erich Fromm (New York: Rinehart and Co., 1947), 126–33. Copyright © 1947, 1975 by Erich Fromm. Reprinted by permission of Henry Holt and Company, Inc.

"The Humanistic Credo" is taken from *Beyond the Chains of Illusion* by Erich Fromm (New York: Simon and Schuster, 1962), 174–82. Copyright © 1962 by Pocket Books, Inc., renewed by the Estate of Erich Fromm. Reprinted by permission of Pocket Books, a division of Simon and Schuster, Inc.

"Authoritarian versus Humanistic Religion" is taken from *Psychoanalysis and Religion* by Erich Fromm (New Haven: Yale University Press, 1950), 34–38. Copyright © 1950 by Erich Fromm. Reprinted by permission of Yale University Press.

"Religious Experience and the Concept of God" is taken from *You Shall Be as Gods: A Radical Interpretation of the Old Testament and Its Tradition* by Erich Fromm (New York: Holt, Rinehart and Winston, 1966), 56–62. Copyright © 1966 by Erich Fromm. Reprinted by permission of Henry Holt and Company, Inc.

"De-Repression and Enlightenment: Psychoanalysis and Zen Buddhism" is taken from *Zen Buddhism and Psychoanalysis* by Erich Fromm (New York: Harper and Row, 1960), 134–41. Copyright © 1960 by Erich Fromm, renewed 1988 by the Estate of Erich Fromm. Reprinted by permission of HarperCollins Publishers.

Introduction by Rainer Funk

An Erich Fromm reader has its own special appeal, and this one has a particular purpose. Erich Fromm is familiar to many as the author of *The Art of Loving* and *To Have or To Be?* but his writings on social psychology, social theory, and religion are much less well known. The main goal of this collection is to introduce the other, unknown Fromm to a wider audience. A second goal is to make readers aware of how *important* these texts are to his thinking, often more so than the best-sellers. Fromm himself was firmly opposed to an approach that would mine his collected writings for nuggets and present them out of context. In compiling this volume, I have taken great care to avoid the simplification or distortion of his ideas as much as possible. Each of the twenty selections is a single connected passage on a central theme in Fromm's thinking. Most of them are concise statements of his insights, ideas, and convictions, but they by no means exhaust the supply of significant texts on each topic.

This collection covers a variety of themes. Many people may be surprised at the breadth of Fromm's interests and the number of subjects on which he wrote. It is my hope that once readers have been introduced to them, they will be stimulated to search out other works.

The selection and arrangement of the texts included in this volume are based on a particular conception. Anyone who attempts to understand Fromm's thinking in its own terms without assigning him overhastily to a particular school will discover a strand of inner logic connecting the many themes in his work. This logic allows us to comprehend why Fromm, a psychoanalyst and social psychologist, also felt compelled to take stands on political, religious, ethical, philosophical, and social questions. One must first grasp Fromm's psychoanalytic and psychological premises, however, to be able to recognize this logical thread. For this reason, the volume begins with the texts on the methods of social psychology and Fromm's theory of character; the other selections build on this groundwork.

Each section is preceded by a short introduction in which I have tried to place the passages in a thematic, biographical, and bibliographical context. I provide titles for the various sections and passages, partly to indicate that some of the selections have been slightly edited and abridged.

Omissions from the original are always marked, however, by [. . .]. A few footnotes in the original have been retained; the rest have been either incorporated into the main text or omitted.

Above all, it is my hope that this volume will succeed in acquainting readers with Fromm as the founder of a humanistic science of humankind and in inspiring them to reflect on and practice his ideas.

PART I

Studying the Social Unconscious

The question of what connects people to one another and what permits them to think, feel, and act jointly is the most important and the most personal scholarly question that Erich Fromm posed. He first formulated it in sociological terms for his dissertation as a student at the University of Heidelberg. Raised in an Orthodox Jewish family in Frankfurt, Fromm decided to investigate the "social glue" that had held Jews together in the Diaspora. He found the answer in the ethos of the Jewish law.

At about the same time, in the years 1923–24, Frieda Reichmann (who later became Fromm's first wife) introduced him to another new branch of science that could offer useful approaches to answering the same question: psychoanalysis as developed by Sigmund Freud. Fromm applied it to inquire into the unconscious forces at work in the minds of human beings not only as individuals but also as social beings. To Fromm, understanding individuals as social creatures meant investigating the social aspect of the unconscious. This was his decisive contribution to psychoanalytic thinking. He combined psychoanalysis and sociology to create an analytic social psychology, which views human beings simultaneously in terms of both their particular social identity and their unconscious determination.

Analytic social psychology does more than permit one to understand the psychic structure of individuals as social beings, however. It allows one to investigate the unconscious of social entities, for social entities consist of individuals who form a society or group because they share an outlook or attitudes. Here Fromm takes the concept of dynamic character as developed by Freud and applies it to social entities. He studies the psychic structure of a society by trying to grasp the society's character as an ideal type. The idea of investigating the social unconscious with the aid of the social character is Fromm's most important contribution to the field of psychology. It also determined Fromm's other interests. Unless one grasps that Fromm approached all other questions from his dominant interest in analytic social psychology, it is difficult to understand his thinking. Whether he is speaking of love, of society, or of being as an alternative to having, Fromm always approaches his topic from the perspective of analytic social psychology.

1

The Approach to a Psychoanalytic Social Psychology

It is one of the essential accomplishments of psychoanalysis that it has done away with the false distinction between social psychology and individual psychology. On the one hand, Freud emphasized that there is no individual psychology of man isolated from his social environment, because an isolated man does not exist. Freud knew no *homo psychologicus*, no psychological Robinson Crusoe, like the economic man of classical economic theory. On the contrary, one of Freud's most important discoveries was the understanding of the psychological development of the individual's earliest social relations—those with his parents, brothers, and sisters.

"It is true," Freud wrote,

> ... that individual psychology is concerned with the individual man and explores the paths by which he seeks to find satisfaction for his instinctual impulses; but only rarely and under certain exceptional conditions is individual psychology in a position to disregard the relations of this individual to others. In the individual's mental life someone else is invariably involved, as a model, as an object, as a helper, as an opponent; and so from the very first, individual psychology, in this extended but entirely justifiable sense of the words, is at the same time social psychology as well.[1]

On the other hand, Freud broke radically with the illusion of a social psychology whose object was "the group." For him, "social instinct" was not the object of psychology any more than isolated man was, since it was not an "original and elemental" instinct; rather, he saw "the beginning

1. Sigmund Freud, *Group Psychology and the Analysis of the Ego* (London: Hogarth Press), standard edition, vol. 18, 69.

of the psyche's formation in a narrower circle, such as the family." He has shown that the psychological phenomena operative in the group are to be understood on the basis of the psychic mechanisms operative in the individual, not on the basis of a "group mind" as such.

The difference between individual and social psychology is revealed to be a quantitative and not a qualitative one. Individual psychology takes into account all determinants that have affected the lot of the individual, and in this way arrives at a maximally complete picture of the individual's psychic structure. The more we extend the sphere of psychological investigation—that is, the greater the number of men whose common traits permit them to be grouped—the more we must reduce the extent of our examination of the total psychic structure of the individual members of the group.

The greater, therefore, the number of subjects of an investigation in social psychology, the narrower the insight into the total psychic structure of any individual within the group being studied. If this is not recognized, misunderstandings will easily arise in the evaluation of the results of such investigations. One expects to hear something about the psychic structure of the individual member of a group, but the social-psychological investigation can study only the character matrix common to all members of the group and does not take into account the total character structure of a particular individual. The latter can never be the task of social psychology and is possible only if an extensive knowledge of the individual's development is available. If, for example, in a social-psychological investigation it is asserted that a group changes from an aggressive-hostile attitude toward the father figure to a passive-submissive attitude, this assertion means something different from the same statement when made of an individual in an individual-psychological investigation. In the latter case, it means that this change is true of the individual's total attitude; in the former, it means that it represents an average characteristic common to all the members of the group, which does not necessarily play a central role in the character structure of each individual. The value of social-psychological investigation, therefore, cannot lie in the fact that we acquire from it a full insight into the psychic peculiarities of the individual members, but only in the fact that we can establish those common psychic tendencies that play a decisive role in their social development.

The overcoming of the theoretical opposition between individual and social psychology accomplished by psychoanalysis leads to the judgment that the method of a social-psychological investigation can be essentially the same as the method which psychoanalysis applies in the investigation of the individual psyche. It will, therefore, be wise to consider briefly the essential features of this method, since it is of significance in the present study.

Freud proceeds from the view that in the causes producing neuroses—and the same holds for the instinctual structure of the healthy—an inherited sexual constitution and the events that have been experienced form a complementary series:

> At one end of the series are the extreme cases of which you could say with conviction: these people, in consequence of the singular development of their libido, would have fallen ill in any case, whatever they had experienced and however carefully their lives had been sheltered. At the other end there are the cases, as to which, on the contrary, you would have had to judge that they would certainly have escaped falling ill if their lives had not brought them into this or that situation. In the cases lying within the series a greater or lesser amount of predisposition in the sexual constitution is combined with a lesser or greater amount of detrimental experience in their lives. Their sexual constitution would not have led them into a neurosis if they had not had these experiences, and these experiences would not have had a traumatic effect on them if their libido had been otherwise disposed.[2]

For psychoanalysis, the constitutional element in the psychic structure of the healthy or of the ill person is a factor that must be observed in the psychological investigation of individuals, but it remains intangible. What psychoanalysis is concerned with is experience; the investigation of its influence on emotional development is its primary purpose. Psychoanalysis is aware, of course, that the emotional development of the individual is determined more or less by his constitution; this insight is a presupposition of psychoanalysis, but psychoanalysis itself is concerned exclusively with the investigation of the influence of the individual's life situation on his emotional development. In practice this means that for the psychoanalytic method a maximum knowledge of the individual's history—mainly of his early childhood experiences but certainly not limited to them—is an essential prerequisite. It studies the relation between a person's life pattern and the specific aspects of his emotional development. Without extensive information concerning the individual's life pattern, analysis is impossible. General observation reveals, of course, that certain typical expressions of behavior will indicate typical life patterns. One could surmise corresponding patterns by analogy, but all such inferences would contain an element of uncertainty and would have limited scientific validity. The method of individual psychoanalysis is therefore a delicately "historical" method: the understanding of emotional development on the

2. Sigmund Freud, *A General Introduction to Psychoanalysis* (New York: Liveright Publishing Corp., 1943), 304.

basis of knowledge of the individual's life history.

The method of applying psychoanalysis to groups cannot be different. The common psychic attitudes of the group members are to be understood only on the basis of their common patterns. Just as individual psychoanalytic psychology seeks to understand the individual emotional constellation, so social psychology can acquire an insight into the emotional structure of a group only by an exact knowledge of its life pattern. Social psychology can make assertions only concerning the psychic attitudes common to all; it therefore requires the knowledge of life situations common to all and characteristic for all.

If the method of social psychology is basically no different from that of individual psychology, there is, nevertheless, a difference which must be pointed out.

Whereas psychoanalytic research is concerned primarily with neurotic individuals, social-psychological research is concerned with groups of normal people.

The neurotic person is characterized by the fact that he has not succeeded in adjusting himself psychically to his real environment. Through the fixation of certain emotional impulses, of certain psychic mechanisms which at one time were appropriate and adequate, he comes into conflict with reality. The psychic structure of the neurotic is therefore almost entirely unintelligible without the knowledge of his early childhood experiences, for, due to his neurosis—an expression of his lack of adjustment or of the particular range of infantile fixations—even his position as an adult is determined essentially by that childhood situation. Even for the normal person the experiences of early childhood are of decisive significance. His character, in the broadest sense, is determined by them, and without them it is unintelligible in its totality. But because he has adjusted himself psychically to reality in a higher degree than the neurotic, a much greater part of his psychic structure is understandable than in the case of the neurotic. Social psychology is concerned with normal people, upon whose psychic situation reality has an incomparably greater influence than upon the neurotic. Thus it can forgo even the knowledge of the individual childhood experiences of the various members of the group under investigation; from the knowledge of the socially conditioned life pattern in which these people were situated after the early years of childhood, it can acquire an understanding of the psychic attitudes common to them.

Social psychology wishes to investigate how certain psychic attitudes common to members of a group are related to their common life experiences. It is no more an accident in the case of an individual whether this or that libido direction dominates, whether the Oedipus complex finds this or that outlet, than it is an accident if changes in psychic characteristics occur in the psychic situation of a group, either in the same class of people over a period of time or simultaneously among different classes. It is the task of social psychology to indicate why such changes occur and how they are to be understood on the basis of the experience common to the members of the group.

2

Social Psychology as a Combination of Psychoanalysis and Historical Materialism

The theory of society with which psychoanalysis seems to have both the greatest affinity and also the greatest differences is *historical materialism*.

They seem to have the most points of contact because they both are materialistic sciences. They do not start from "ideas" but from earthly life and needs. They are particularly close in their appraisal of consciousness, which is seen by both as less the driving force behind human behavior than the reflection of other hidden forces. But when it comes to the nature of the factors that truly condition man's consciousness, there seems to be an irreconcilable opposition between the two theories. Historical materialism sees consciousness as the expression of social existence; psychoanalysis sees it as determined by instinctual drives. Certain questions are unavoidable: Do the two views contradict each other? If not, how are they related? Can the use of the psychoanalytic method enrich historical materialism? If so, how? [. . .]

Psychoanalysis [. . .] seeks to know the psychic traits common to the members of a group and to explain these common psychic traits in terms of shared life experiences. These life experiences, however, do not lie in the realm of the personal or the accidental—the larger the group is, the more this holds true—but rather they are identical with the socioeconomic situation of this particular group. *Thus analytical social psychology seeks to understand the instinctual apparatus of a group, its libidinous and largely unconscious behavior, in terms of its socioeconomic structure.* [. . .]

Applying the method of psychoanalytic individual psychology to

From "The Method and Function of an Analytic Social Psychology," in *The Crisis of Psychoanalysis*, by Erich Fromm. Copyright © 1955, 1958, 1963 by Erich Fromm. Reprinted by permission of Henry Holt and Company, Inc.

social phenomena, we find that *the phenomena of social psychology are to be understood as processes involving the active and passive adaptation of the instinctual apparatus to the socioeconomic situation. In certain fundamental respects, the instinctual apparatus itself is a biological given; but it is highly modifiable. The role of primary formative factors goes to the economic conditions. The family is the essential medium through which the economic situation exerts its formative influence on the individual's psyche. The task of social psychology is to explain the shared, socially relevant, psychic attitudes and ideologies—and their unconscious roots in particular—in terms of the influence of economic conditions on libido strivings.*

So far, then, the method of analytic social psychology seems to dovetail with the method of Freudian individual psychology and with the requirements of historical materialism. But new difficulties arise when this method is confused with an erroneous but widespread interpretation of the Marxist theory: the notion that historical materialism is a psychological theory or, more specifically, an economistic psychology. [...]

The idea that the "acquisitive drive" is the basic or only motive of human behavior is the brainchild of bourgeois liberalism, used as a psychological argument against the possibility of the realization of socialism. Marx's petit bourgeois interpreters interpreted his theory as an economistic psychology. In reality, historical materialism is far from being a psychological theory; its psychological presuppositions are few and may be briefly listed: *Men* make their own history; *needs* motivate men's actions and feelings (hunger and love); these needs increase in the course of historical development, thereby spurring increased economic activity.

In connection with psychology, the economic factor plays a role in historical materialism only to the extent that human needs—primarily the need for self-preservation—are largely satisfied through the production of goods; in short, needs are the lever that stimulates production. Marx and Engels certainly stressed that the drive toward self-preservation took priority over all other needs, but they did not go into any detail about the quality of various drives and needs. However, they never maintained that the "acquisitive drive," the passion for acquisition as an aim in itself, was the only or essential need. To proclaim it a universal human drive would be naively to absolutize a psychic trait that has taken on uncommon force in capitalist society. [...]

When the materialistic view of history talks about economic causes [...] it is not talking about economics as a subjective psychological motive but as an objective influence on man's activity in life. All man's activity, the satisfying of all his needs, depends on the specific nature of natural economic conditions around; and it is these conditions that determine how man shall live his life. For Marx, man's consciousness is to be explained in terms of his existence in society, in terms of his real, earthly life that is conditioned by the state of his productive capabilities. [. . .]

Psychoanalysis can enrich the overall conception of historical materialism on one specific point. *It can provide a more comprehensive knowledge of one of the factors that is operative in the social process: the nature of man himself.* It locates man's instinctual apparatus among the natural factors that modify the social process, although there are also limits to this modifiability. Man's instinctual apparatus is one of the "natural" conditions that forms part of the substructure (*Unterbau*) of the social process. But we are not talking about the instinctual apparatus "in general," or in some pristine biological form, since it is only manifest in some *specific* form that has been modified through the social process. The human psyche—or the libidinal forces as its root—is part of the substructure; but it is not the whole substructure, as a psychologistic interpretation would have it. The human psyche always remains a psyche that has been modified by the social process. Historical materialism calls for a psychology—i.e., a science of man's psychic structure—and psychoanalysis is the first discipline to provide a psychology that historical materialism can really use.

The contribution of psychoanalysis is particularly important for the following reasons. Marx and Engels postulated the dependence of all ideological processes on the economic substructure. They saw intellectual and psychic creations as "the material basis reflected in man's head." In many instances, to be sure, historical materialism could provide the right answers without any psychological presuppositions. But only where ideology was the *immediate* expression of economic interests; or where one was trying to establish the correlation between economic substructure and ideological superstructure. Lacking a satisfactory psychology, Marx and Engels could not explain *how* the material basis was reflected in man's head and heart.

Psychoanalysis can show that man's ideologies are the products of certain wishes, instinctual drives, interests, and needs, which themselves, in large measure, unconsciously find expression as rationalizations—i.e., as ideologies. Psychoanalysis can show that while the instinctual drives do develop on the basis of biologically determined instincts, their quantity and content are greatly affected by the individual's socioeconomic situation or class. Marx says that men are the producers of their ideologies; analytical social psychology can describe empirically the process of the production of ideologies, of the interaction of "natural" and social factors. *Hence psychoanalysis can show how the economic situation is transformed into ideology via man's drives.*

An important point to note is the fact that this interaction between instincts and environment results in changes within man himself, just as his work changes extra-human nature. Here we can only suggest the general direction of this change. It involves, as Freud has stressed repeatedly, the growth of man's ego organization and the corresponding growth of his capacity for sublimation. Thus psychoanalysis permits us to regard the formation of ideologies as a type of "production process," as another form of the "metabolism" between man and nature. The distinctive aspect here is that "nature" is also within man, not just outside him.

Psychoanalysis can also tell us something about the way ideologies or ideas mold society. It can show that the impact of an idea depends essentially on its unconscious content, which appeals to certain drives; that it is, as it were, the quality and intensity of the libidinal structure of a society which determine the social effect of an ideology. [...]

The fruitfulness of a psychoanalytic social psychology will depend, of course, on the significance of the libidinal forces in the social process. We could not even begin to treat this topic thoroughly in this article, so I shall content myself with a few basic suggestions and indications.

Suppose we ask which forces maintain the stability of a given society and which undermine it. We can see that economic prosperity and social conflicts determine stability or decomposition, respectively. But we can also see that the factor which, on the basis of these conditions, serves as a most important element in the social structure is the libidinal tendencies actually operative in men. Consider first a relatively stable social constellation. What holds people together? What enables them to have a certain feeling of solidarity, to adjust to the role of ruling or being ruled? To be sure, it is the external power apparatus (police, law courts, army, etc.) that keeps the society from coming apart at the seams. To be sure, it is rational and egotistic interests that contribute to structural stability. But neither the external power apparatus nor rational interests would suffice to guarantee the functioning of the society if the libidinal strivings of the people were not involved. They serve as the "cement," as it were, without which the society would not hold together, and which contributes to the production of important social ideologies in every cultural sphere.

Let us apply this principle to an especially important social constellation: class relationships. In history as we know it, a minority rules over the majority of society. This class rule was not the result of cunning and deceit, but was a necessary result of the total economic situation of society, of its productive forces. As Necker saw it: "Through the laws of property, the proletariat were condemned to get the barest minimum for their labor." Or, as Linguet put it, they were "to a certain extent, a conspiracy against the majority of the human race, who could find no recourse against them."[1]

The Enlightenment described and criticized this dependency relationship, even though it did not realize that it was economically conditioned. Indeed, minority rule is a historical fact; but what factors allowed this dependency relationship to become stabilized?

First, of course, it was the use of physical force and the availability of these physical means to certain groups. But there was another important factor at work: the libidinal ties—anxiety, love, trust—which filled the souls of the majority in their relationships with the ruling class. Now this psychic attitude is not the product of whim or accident. It is the expression of people's libidinal adaptation to the conditions of life imposed by economic necessity. So long as these conditions necessitate minority rule over the majority, the libido adapts itself to this economic structure and serves as one of the factors that lend stability to the class relationship.

Besides recognizing the *economic conditions* of the libido structure, social psychology should not forget to investigate the *psychological basis* of this structure. It must explore not only why this libido structure necessarily exists but also how it is psychologically possible and through what mechanisms it operates. Exploring the roots of the majority's libidinal ties to the ruling minority, social psychology might discover that this tie is a repetition or continuation of the child's psychic attitude toward his parents, particularly toward his father, in a bourgeois family. We find a mixture of admiration, fear, faith, and confidence in the father's strength and wisdom, briefly, an affectively conditioned reflection of his intellectual and moral qualities, and we find the same in adults of a patriarchal class society vis-à-vis the members of the ruling class. Related to this are certain moral principles which entice the poor to suffer rather than to do wrong, and which lead them to believe that the purpose of their life is to obey their rulers and do their duty. Even these ethical conceptions, which are so important for social stability, are the products of certain affective and emotional relations to those who create and represent such norms.

To be sure, the creation of these norms is not left to chance. One whole basic part of the cultural apparatus serves to form the socially required attitude in a systematic and methodical way. It is an important task of social psychology to analyze the function of the whole educational system and other systems (such as the penal system) in this process.

We have focused on the libidinal relationships between the ruling minority and the ruled majority because this factor is the social and psychic

---

1. Cited by K. Grünberg, "Verhandlungen der Generalversammlung des Vereins fur Sozialpolitik (Leipzig: Duncker & Humblot, 1924), p. 31.

core of every class society. But other social relationships, too, bear their own distinctive libidinal stamp. The relationships between members of the same class have a different psychic coloring in the lower middle class than they do in the proletariat. Or, the relationship to the political leader is different, for example, in the case of a proletarian leader who identifies with his class and serves their interests even while he leads them, from what it is when he confronts them as a strong man, as the great father who rules as omnipotent authority.

The diversity of possible libidinal relationships is matched by the wide variety of possible emotional relationships within society. Even a brief sketch is impossible here; this problem would, indeed, be a major task for an analytic social psychology. Let me just point out that every society has its own distinctive *libidinal structure*, even as it has its own economic, social, political, and cultural structure. This libidinal structure is the product of the influence of socioeconomic conditions on human drives; in turn, it is an important factor conditioning emotional developments within the various levels of society, and the contents of the "ideological superstructure." The libidinal structure of a society is the medium through which the economy exerts its influence on man's intellectual and mental manifestations. (What I have called here the "libidinal structure of society," using Freudian terminology, I have in my later work called the "social character"; in spite of the change in the libido theory, the concepts are the same.)

Of course, the libidinal structure of a society does not remain constant, no more than does its economic and social structure. But it remains relatively constant so long as the social structure retains a certain equilibrium—i.e., during the phase of relative consolidation in the society's development. With the growth of objective contradictions and conflicts within the society, and with the acceleration of the disintegration process, certain changes in the society's libidinal structure also take place. We see the disappearance of traditional ties that maintained the stability of the society; there is change in traditional emotional attitudes. Libidinal energies are freed for new uses, and thus change their social function. They no longer serve the preservation of the society, but contribute to the development of new social formations. They cease to be "cement," and turn into dynamite. [...]

Clearly, analytic psychology has its place within the framework of historical materialism. It investigates one of the natural factors that is operative in the relationship between society and nature: the realm of human drives, and the active and passive role they play within the social process. Thus it investigates a factor that plays a decisive mediating role between the economic base and the formation of ideologies. Thus analytic social psychology enables us to understand fully the ideological superstructure in terms of the process that goes on between society and man's nature.

Now we can readily summarize the findings of our study on the method and function of a psychoanalytic social psychology. Its method is that of classical Freudian psychoanalysis as applied to social phenomena. It explains the shared, socially relevant, psychic attitudes in terms of the process of active and passive adaptation of the apparatus of drives to the socioeconomic living conditions of the society.

Its task is, first of all, to analyze the socially relevant libidinal strivings: i.e., to describe the libidinal structure of a given society, and to explain the origin of this structure and its function in the social process. An important element of this work, then, will be the theory explaining how ideologies arise from the interaction of the psychic apparatus and the socioeconomic conditions.

3

The Dynamic Concept of Character

The behavioristic view is that behavior is the ultimately attainable and at the same time scientifically satisfactory datum in the study of man. From this standpoint, behavior traits and character traits are identical, and from a positivistic standpoint, even the concept "character" may not be legitimate in scientific parlance.

From the psychoanalytic standpoint, a character trait is an energy-charged part of the whole system-character, which can be understood fully only if one understands the whole system. Character traits are the roots of behavior traits, and one character trait may express itself in one or more different behavior traits; its existence may not be conscious, but it can be inferred from various phenomena (like small details of behavior, dreams, etc.).

Behavior, which is essentially an adaptation to realistic circumstances, changes relatively easily when circumstances make another kind of behavior more advisable; character traits usually persist even when they become harmful under changed circumstances (especially neurotic character traits).

The discovery of the dynamic concept of character was undoubtedly one of Freud's greatest contributions to the science of man. He had begun to develop it in his first paper on the anal character (1908). The essential point of that paper was that certain behavior traits, namely stubbornness, orderliness, and parsimony, were more often than not to be found together as a syndrome of traits. Furthermore, wherever that syndrome existed, one could find peculiarities in the sphere of toilet training and in the vicissitudes of sphincter control and in certain behavioral traits related to bowel movements and feces. Thus, Freud's first step was to discover a syndrome of behavioral traits and to relate them to the way the child acted (in part as a response to certain demands by those who trained him) in the sphere of bowel movements and elimination. His brilliant and creative step was to relate these two sets of behavioral complexes by a theoretical consideration based on a previous assumption about the evolution of the libido. This assumption was that during an early phase of childhood development, after the mouth has ceased to be the main organ of lust and satisfaction, the anus becomes an important erogenous zone, and most libidinal wishes are centered around the process of the retention and evacuation of the excrements. His next conclusion was to explain the syndrome of behavioral traits as sublimation of, or reaction formation against, the libidinous satisfaction or frustration of anality. Stubbornness and parsimony were supposed to be the sublimation of the original refusal to give up the pleasure of retaining the stool; orderliness the reaction formation against the original desire of the infant to evacuate wherever he pleased. In this story Freud gave an explanation for the traits which were part of the original anal syndrome, which was later enlarged to comprise a number of other traits. (Traits which were added later to the original syndrome are exaggerated cleanliness and punctuality; they are also to be understood as reaction formations to the original anal impulses.) Freud showed that the three original traits of the syndrome, which until then appeared to be quite unrelated among each other, formed part of a structure or system, because they were all rooted in the same source of anal libido, which manifests itself in these traits either directly or by reaction formation or sublimation. In this way Freud was able to explain why these traits are charged with energy and, in fact, very resistant to change. In principle the same procedure was applied to the study of the oral-receptive and the oral-sadistic character and to the concept of the genital character. The most important later addition to the concept of the anal character was the assumption that sadistic behavior was also part of the anal syndrome.

The fruitfulness of this new dynamic concept of character for the study of individual or social behavior is immediately apparent. A simple example will tend to clarify this: If a person is poor, his behavior may be a hoarding or stingy one; that is to say, he shows great reluctance to make any but the most necessary expenditures. This can, of course, be a behavioral trait responding to the necessities of the realistic situation. A poor person is forced to behave that way if he is to survive. Should his economic situation improve, he would also change his behavior accordingly and no longer insist on avoiding any expense which is not absolutely necessary. We call such a person thrifty or parsimonious. However, when parsimoniousness is a character trait it exists regardless of the economic circumstances of the person. When we speak of this type of a characterologically thrifty person we speak of a "miser," and by this we refer to his character rather than only to thrifty behavior. As long as such a person is poor, one will of course be prone to explain his behavior as a reaction to his poverty. But such an explanation fails if the miser, having become rich, continues to act according to his previous pattern.

That miserliness as a character trait is not learned, nor an adaptive response, is borne out by the following considerations: (1) Miserliness is to be found among people for whom it was never adaptive and who never learned it. (2) The miser acts according to the hoarding principle not only with regard to material things, where savings might be rationalized as being useful, but also to save his physical, sexual, or mental energy, because he feels any expenditure of energy as a loss. (3) When the miser acts true to his pattern he experiences a strong satisfaction, which can even sometimes be observed in his smug facial expression. (4) Any attempt to change his behavior pattern meets with great difficulties (resistance). Many a miser who lives in a milieu where miserly behavior is unpopular would love to change his behavior pattern, yet often he cannot. If this were only a matter of learned behavior this difficulty would be hard to understand. But it becomes very understandable if one thinks of it as a trait charged with energy, which is part of a character system and which could change only if the whole system changed. If the behaviorist point were right, then it would be indeed difficult to understand why individuals or classes often act against their own interests, even against their interest in survival, when rationally and realistically alternative behavior patterns are at hand. In fact, all the irrational passions of man, of which history is a sad record, are nonadaptive and even harmful. The frequent inability of societies to change their traditional character traits for the sake of adaptive ones is one of the causes of their destruction.

Courage may serve as another example for the difference between behavior trait and character trait. Courage as behavior trait might thus be described: a behavior of a person who in the pursuit of an aim is not easily deterred by danger to life, health, freedom, or property. Such a definition covers virtually all kinds of courageous behavior.

The picture, however, is different if we take into account the motivation—often unconscious—of acting courageously. A courageous person (for instance, a soldier in a war) can be motivated by dedication to his goal or sense of duty, and we usually have this motivation in mind when we speak of courage as being a virtue. But courage can also be motivated by vanity, the wish for recognition and admiration; or by suicidal tendencies in which loss of life might be desired even though unconsciously; or by lack of imagination, which makes the individual blind to dangers; or by the fear of being considered a coward; or by liquor; or by all or any of these motivations blended with each other.

Are individuals aware of their motivation? Whatever the motive of the person who behaves courageously, he will usually assume that he is motivated by dedication or duty, and so will those who witness his behavior. In cases where the motivating force is not dedication but a less noble impulse, the real motivation is more likely to remain unconscious.

Is the behavior the same, regardless of the different motivations? On the surface it seems to be the same, but a detailed analysis of the behavior will show that this is not so. Let us take as an example an army officer in charge of a company. If he is motivated by a sense of dedication to a goal or by a sense of duty, he will take risks and demand that his soldiers take risks, which are in proportion to the importance of the tactical goals. If, on the other hand, he is motivated by vanity or suicidal tendencies, he will risk the lives of his soldiers (and his own life) unnecessarily; he may even disobey orders from his superiors and thus do harm to the general tactical or strategic plans. Differences in the motivation of leading generals and politicians might spell the difference between life and death for the nations they lead.

One important difference between behavior traits and character traits needs to be stressed. The behavior trait is an adaptive response to a given social situation and is essentially the result of learning. For this reason, as we have already said, behavior traits can change relatively easily when conditions change.

Character traits, on the other hand, are part of a dynamic system, the system-character. They change only inasmuch as the whole system changes, but not independently. The system as a whole has been formed in response to the total social configuration; however, this response is not an arbitrary one but conditioned by the nature of man, which determines the ways in which human energy can be channeled. *The system-character is the relatively permanent form in which human energy is structuralized in the process of relating to others and of assimilating nature.* It is the result of dynamic interaction of the system-man and the system-society in which he lives.

It is precisely this systemic, structural quality which is essential in Freud's character concept. It may be that for this very reason it has not found the full understanding and recognition it deserves. It is to be hoped that the recent interest in systems and structure will also lead to a new appreciation of the psychoanalytic concept of character.

The significance of the dynamic concept of character becomes even clearer when looked upon from a sociobiological rather than from Freud's mechanistic-physiological standpoint. The instinctive determination of actions is weaker in man than in all other animals. In fact, instinctive behavior hardly exists in man. Like other animals, man has to act and to make decisions, but unlike other animals he cannot make these decisions automatically, because his instincts do not determine his decisions. If, on the other hand, every decision were made on the basis of conscious deliberation, an individual would be overwhelmed by information and by doubt. Many vital decisions have to be made in a time range much shorter than a deliberation of what is best would require. Character in the dynamic sense *becomes a substitute for instinct*. The person with what Freud calls an "anal character" will "instinctively" hoard, shy away from expenditures, and act strongly against any menace to his possessions. He does not have to *think* about these reactions because his character-system makes him act spontaneously without having to think, in spite of the fact that his actions are not determined by instinct.

A further significant function of character in the dynamic sense is that it unifies a person's action. The anal character who tends to be hoarding, punctual, overclean, suspicious, and constantly on the defensive has built up an integrated system which has its own logic and order. He is not stingy today and magnanimous tomorrow, or cold and closed today and warm and open tomorrow. In other words, because of the unifying nature of a system, constant friction between various tendencies is avoided. This friction would exist if a person were to make each of his choices consciously and as a result of deliberation or mood. This function of unification is important, because otherwise the friction of conflicting tendencies would result in a marked waste of energy within the whole system; in fact, living would be rather precarious.

Having pointed out the significance of Freud's discovery of the dynamic concept of character, we must add that of course this concept was by no means unknown before Freud. From Heraclitus, who said, "character is man's fate," to Greek and Shakespearean drama, to Balzac's novels, we find the same concept of character, namely that man is driven to act the way he acts, that there are several systems of character which lead to different actions, and that one can understand personality only if one understands the system underlying man's behavior. But Freud was the first scientist and psychologist who elaborated on the concept of character in a scientific way and who laid the foundations for a systematic study of character structure.

Even though the concept of character [...] is built on these foundations, it differs with respect to a number of theoretical elements which formed part of Freud's original theory.

To begin with, we do not consider that instinct mediates human relationships. For instance, the infant's bond to the mother is not primarily based on satisfaction of the sucking instinct, but has to be understood in a much wider sense. While to give sucking satisfaction is one of the mother's functions, there are other functions which are more important, as, for example, skin contact. But still more important is the factor of unconditional love, which has nothing to do with a specific need, but rather with the quality of the whole relationship of mother to infant. Mother is always there, always ready to help, always ready to alleviate discomfort, to respond. She mediates all of reality; she *is* reality, she is the world; she is the comforting, all-reliable goddess—at least in the first years of the child's life. The crucial question is not the mechanistic one of which instincts are satisfied, but the sociobiological one: which function the mother has in and for the total life process of the infant at a given point of its development.

Freud's clinical descriptions of the oral-receptive, oral-exploitative, and anal character seem to us essentially correct and confirmed by experiences in the analysis of individuals, as well as analytical research into the character structure of groups. The difference lies not in the *description* of the character syndrome but in its *theoretical explanation*, which has some significant consequences for the application of the character syndromes, as Freud found them in the individual, to understanding social character. As we already pointed out, Freud's guiding theoretical concepts referred to the vicissitudes in the evolution of libido. His stages of character development follow the stages of libido development in the sense that their sequence was the same, and furthermore that the energy with which the character syndrome is charged is derived from the sexual energy vested in the corresponding pregenital erogenous zones.

We, on the other hand, start out from a sociobiological question: What kind of ties to the world, persons and things, must—and can—man develop in order to survive, given his specific equipment and the nature of the world around him? Man has to fulfill two functions in order to survive. First, he has to provide for his material needs (food, shelter, etc.) and for the survival needs of the group in terms of procreation and protection of the young. We have called this "the process of assimilation" and have pointed out in *Man for Himself* (1947) that there are only certain specific ways in which man can assimilate things for his own use: either by receiving them passively (receptive character), by taking them by force (exploitative character), by hoarding whatever he has (hoarding character), or by producing through work that which he needs (productive character). However, man being endowed with self-awareness, with a need to choose, to plan, and to foresee dangers and difficulties, and being uprooted from his original home within nature by the absence of instinctive determination, could not remain sane even if he took care of all his material needs, unless he were able to establish some form of relatedness to others that allows him to feel "at home" and saves him from the experience of complete affective isolation and separateness, which is in fact the basis of severe mental sickness. (To relate oneself is also a social necessity because no social organization could exist unless the members of the organization had some feeling of relatedness among themselves.) Man, inasmuch as he is an animal, is driven to avoid death, while man *qua* man is driven to avoid madness. This he does by means of various forms of relating himself, in the "process of socialization." He can relate himself to others in a symbiotic way (sadistically or masochistically), in purely destructive ways, in a narcissistic way, and in a loving way. [. . .]

Both the process of assimilation and the process of socialization have as their aim not only survival (physical and psychic) but also the expression of man's potential by the active use of his physical, affective, and intellectual powers. In this process of becoming what he potentially is, man expresses his energies in the most adequate way. When he cannot express his self actively, he suffers, is passive, and tends to become sick.

To sum up: In talking about the receptive, exploitative, hoarding, and productive orientations we do not refer to a form of relatedness to the world which is mediated by certain forms of the sexual instinct, but to forms of relatedness of the human being to the world in the process of living.

This conceptual change leads also to a change in the concept of energy, with which the character system is charged. For Freud this energy was the sexual energy, libido. From our theoretical standpoint it is the energy within a total living organism which tends to survive and to express itself. There is no need to speak of "desexualized energy," which is a discovery only if one started with an orthodox viewpoint. Descriptively, we use the generalized concept of energy similar to the use of "libido" by C. G. Jung.

Freud's concept of character was developed by clinical observation of individuals, not of groups. Furthermore, he saw the basis for the development of the individual character in another "private" phenomenon—the individual family. He did not apply his concepts of character to societies or classes.

This statement does not imply that Freud's theory lacked a social orientation. He was very aware that individual psychology can rarely neglect the relationship of one individual to another and that—as he wrote in *Group Psychology and the Analysis of the Ego* (1922)—"individual psychology is from the very beginning at the same time social psychology in the enlarged but completely legitimate sense." He went even further. He speculated upon the possibilities of collective neuroses and concluded this speculation with the following statement: "In spite of these difficulties we may expect that one day someone will venture upon this research into the pathology of civilized communities." But in spite of these speculations Freud never went beyond the study of the individual character and its roots in the individual family.

4

The Social Character and Its Functions

In studying the psychological reactions of a social group we deal with the character structure of the members of the group, that is, of individual persons; we are interested, however, not in the peculiarities by which these persons differ from each other, but in that part of their character structure that is common to most members of the group. We can call this character the *social character*. The social character necessarily is less specific than the individual character. In describing the latter we deal with the whole of the traits which in their particular configuration form the personality structure of this or that individual. The social character comprises only a selection of traits, *the essential nucleus of the character structure of most members of a group which has developed as the result of the basic experiences and mode of life common to that group.* Although there will be always "deviants" with a totally different character structure, the character structures of most members of the group are variations of this nucleus, brought about by the accidental factors of birth and life experience as they differ from one individual to another. If we want to understand one individual most fully, these differentiating elements are of the greatest importance. However, if we want to understand how human energy is channeled and operates as a productive force in a given social order, then the social character deserves our main interest.

The concept of social character is a key concept for the understanding of the social process. Character in the dynamic sense of analytic psychology is the specific form in which human energy is shaped by the dynamic adaptation of human needs to the particular mode of existence of a given society. Character in its turn determines the thinking, feeling, and acting of individuals. To see this is somewhat difficult with regard to our thoughts, since we all tend to share the conventional belief that thinking is an exclusively intellectual act and independent of the psychological structure of the personality. This is not so, however, and the less so the more our thoughts deal with ethical, philosophical, political, psychological, or social problems rather than with the empirical manipulation of concrete objects. Such thoughts, aside from the purely logical elements that are involved in the act of thinking, are greatly determined by the personality structure of the person who thinks. This holds true for the whole of a doctrine or of a theoretical system as well as for a single concept, like love, justice, equality, sacrifice. Each such concept and each doctrine has an emotional matrix, and this matrix is rooted in the character structure of the individual. [. . .]

Although the word which two people of different personality use when they speak of love, for instance, is the same, the meaning of the word is entirely different according to their character structure. As a matter of fact, much intellectual confusion could be avoided by correct psychological analysis of the meaning of these concepts, since any attempt at a purely logical classification must necessarily fail.

The fact that ideas have an emotional matrix is of the utmost importance because it is the key to the understanding of the spirit of a culture. Different societies or classes within a society have a specific social character, and on its basis different ideas develop and become powerful. Thus, for instance, the idea of work and success as the main aims of life were able to become powerful and appealing to modern man on the basis of his aloneness and doubt; but propaganda for the idea of ceaseless effort and striving for success addressed to the Pueblo Indians or to Mexican peasants would fall completely flat. These people with a different kind of character structure would hardly understand what a person setting forth such aims was talking about even if they understood his language. In the same way, Hitler and that part of the German population which has the same character structure quite sincerely feel that anybody who thinks that wars can be abolished is either a complete fool or a plain liar. On the basis of their social character, to them life without suffering and disaster is as little comprehensible as freedom and equality.

Ideas often are consciously accepted by certain groups, which, on account of the peculiarities of their social character, are not really touched by them; such ideas remain a stock of conscious convictions, but people fail to act according to them in a critical hour. An example of this is shown in the German labor movement at the time of the victory of Nazism. The vast majority of German workers before Hitler's coming into power voted for the Socialist or Communist parties and believed in the ideas of those parties; that is, the *range* of these ideas among the working class was extremely wide. The *weight* of these ideas, however, was in no proportion to their range. The onslaught of Nazism did not meet with political opponents, the majority of whom were ready to fight for their ideas. Many of the adherents of the leftist parties, although they believed in their party programs as long as the parties had authority, were ready to resign when the hour of crisis arrived. A close analysis of the character structure of German workers can show one reason—certainly not the only one—for this phenomenon. A great number of them were of a personality type that has many of the traits of what we have described as the authoritarian character. They had a deep-seated respect and longing for established authority. The emphasis of socialism on individual independence versus authority, on solidarity versus individualistic seclusion, was not what many of these workers really wanted on the basis of their personality structure. One mistake of the radical leaders was to estimate the strength of their parties only on the basis of the range which these ideas had, and to overlook their lack of weight.

In contrast to this picture, the analysis of Protestant and Calvinist doctrines can show that those ideas were powerful forces within the adherents of the new religion, because they appealed to needs and anxieties that were present in the character structure of the people to whom they were addressed. In other words, *ideas can become powerful forces, but only to the extent to which they are answers to specific human needs prominent in a given social character.*

Not only thinking and feeling are determined by man's character structure but also his actions. It is Freud's achievement to have shown this, even if his theoretical frame of reference is incorrect. The determinations of activity by the dominant trends of a person's character structure are obvious in the case of neurotics. It is easy to understand that the compulsion to count the windows of houses and the number of stones on the pavement is an activity that is rooted in certain drives of the compulsive character. But the actions of a normal person appear to be determined only by rational considerations and the necessities of reality. However, with the new tools of observation that psychoanalysis offers, we can recognize that so-called rational behavior is largely determined by the character structure. [...]

We have now to ask what function character serves for the individual and for society. As to the former the answer is not difficult. If an individual's character more or less closely conforms with the social character, the dominant drives in his personality lead him to do what is necessary and desirable under the specific social conditions of his culture. Thus, for instance, if he has a passionate drive to save and an abhorrence of spending money for any luxury, he will be greatly helped by this drive—supposing he is a small shopkeeper who needs to save and to be thrifty if he wants to survive. Besides this economic function, character traits have a purely psychological one which is no less important. The person with whom saving is a desire springing from his personality gains also a profound psychological satisfaction in being able to act accordingly; that is, he is not only benefited practically when he saves, but he also feels satisfied psychologically. One can easily convince oneself of this if one observes, for instance, a woman of the lower middle class shopping in the market and being as happy about two cents saved as another person of a different character may be about the enjoyment of some sensuous pleasure. This psychological satisfaction occurs not only if a person acts in accordance with the demands springing from his character structure but also when he reads or listens to ideas that appeal to him for the same reason. For the authoritarian character, an ideology that describes nature as the powerful force to which we have to submit, or a speech which indulges in sadistic descriptions of political occurrences, has a profound attraction, and the act of reading or listening results in psychological satisfaction. To sum up: The subjective function of character for the normal person is to *lead him to act according to what is necessary for him from a practical standpoint and also to give him satisfaction from his activity psychologically.*

If we look at social character from the standpoint of its function in the social process, we have to start with the statement that has been made with regard to its function for the individual: that by adapting himself to social conditions man develops those traits that make him *desire* to act as he *has* to act. If the character of the majority of people in a given society— that is, the social character—is thus adapted to the objective tasks the individual has to perform in this society, the energies of people are molded in ways that make them into productive forces that are indispensable for the functioning of that society. Let us take up once more the example of work. Our modern industrial system requires that most of our energy be channeled in the direction of work. Were it only that people worked because of external necessities, much friction between what they ought to do and what they would like to do would arise and lessen their efficiency. However, by the dynamic adaptation of character to social requirements, human energy instead of causing friction is shaped into such forms as to become an incentive to act according to the particular economic necessities. Thus modern man, instead of having to be forced to work as hard as he does, is driven by the inner compulsion to work. [. . .] Or, instead of obeying overt authorities, he has built up an inner authority—conscience and duty—which operates more effectively in controlling him than any external authority could ever do. In other words, *the social character internalizes external necessities and thus harnesses human energy for the task of a given economic and social system.*

As we have seen, once certain needs have developed in a character structure, any behavior in line with these needs is at the same time satisfactory psychologically and practical from the standpoint of material success. As long as a society offers the individual those two satisfactions simultaneously, we have a situation where the psychological forces are *cementing* the social structure. Sooner or later, however, a lag arises. The traditional character structure still exists while new economic conditions have arisen, for which the traditional character traits are no longer useful. People tend to act according to their character structure, but either these actions are actual handicaps in their economic pursuits or there is not enough opportunity for them to find positions that allow them to act according to their "nature." An illustration of what we have in mind is the character structure of the old middle classes, particularly in countries with a rigid class stratification like Germany. The old middle-class virtues—frugality, thrift, cautiousness, suspiciousness—were of diminishing value in modern business in comparison with new virtues, such as initiative, a readiness to take risks, aggressiveness, and so on. Even inasmuch as these old virtues were still an asset—as with the small shopkeeper—the range of possibilities for such business was so narrowed down that only a minority of the sons of the old middle class could "use" their character traits successfully in their economic pursuits. While by their upbringing they had developed character traits that once were adapted to the social situation of their class, the economic development went faster than the character development. This lag between economic and psychological evolution resulted in a situation in which the psychic needs could no longer be satisfied by the usual economic activities. These needs existed, however, and had to seek for satisfaction in some other way. Narrow egotistical striving for one's own advantage, as it had characterized the lower middle class, was shifted from the individual plane to that of the nation. The sadistic impulses, too, that had been used in the battle of private competition were partly shifted to the social and political scene, and partly intensified by frustration. Then, freed from any restricting factors, they sought satisfaction in acts of political persecution and war. Thus, blended with the resentment caused by the frustrating qualities of the whole situation, the psychological forces instead of cementing the existing social order became dynamite to be used by groups which wanted to destroy the traditional political and economic structure of democratic society.

We have not spoken of the role which the educational process plays with regard to the formation of the social character; but in view of the fact that to many psychologists the methods of early childhood training and the educational techniques employed toward the growing child appear to be the *cause* of character development, some remarks on this point seem to be warranted. In the first place we should ask ourselves what we mean by education. While education can be defined in various ways, the way to look at it from the angle of the social process seems to be something like this. The social function of education is to qualify the individual to function in the role he is to play later on in society; that is, to mold his character in such a way that it approximates the social character, that his desires coincide with the necessities of his social role. The educational system of any society is determined by this function; therefore we cannot *explain* the structure of society or the personality of its members by the educational process; but we have to explain the educational system by the necessities resulting from the social and economic structure of a given society. However, the methods of education are extremely important insofar as they are the mechanisms by which the individual is molded into the required shape. They can be considered as the means by which social requirements are transformed into personal qualities. While educational techniques are not the cause of a particular kind of social character, they constitute one of the mechanisms by which character is formed. In this sense, the knowledge and understanding of educational methods is an important part of the total analysis of a functioning society.

What we have just said also holds true for one particular sector of the whole educational process: the *family*. Freud has shown that the early experiences of the child have a decisive influence upon the formation of its character structure. If this is true, how then can we understand that the child, who—at least in our culture—has little contact with the life of society, is molded by it? The answer is not only that the parents—aside from certain individual variations—apply the educational patterns of the society they live in, but also that in their own personalities they represent the social character of their society or class. They transmit to the child what we may call the psychological atmosphere or the spirit of a society just by being as they are—namely representatives of this very spirit. *The family thus may be considered to be the psychological agent of society.*

PART II

The Discovery of Different Social Characters

Fromm's concern is with the unconscious psychic structure of social entities. To pursue this interest (and to become a practicing analyst), he spent the years between 1924 and 1930 in psychoanalytic training in Munich, Frankfurt, and Berlin. His continuing interest in analytic social psychology also led him to accept an invitation from Max Horkheimer in 1930 to join the Institute for Social Research in Frankfurt. Until 1939 he devoted himself as a member of the "Frankfurt school" mainly to a study of the authoritarian psychic structure of social entities, thus creating the basis for a lengthy scholarly debate on authority and authoritarianism.

Fromm was convinced that development of the psychic structure of social entities, i.e., the social character, depends on social and economic structures. He saw this demonstrated with particular clarity in the case of the marketing character. He began to identify this structure as a conformist and escapist mechanism in the 1940s in his book *Escape from Freedom* and identified it as the marketing character in *Man for Himself: An Inquiry into the Psychology of Ethics* (1947).

Fromm became aware of a further orientation of the social character in the early sixties, an orientation that he termed *necrophilia*. He first described this phenomenon in 1964 in his book *The Heart of Man* and went on to consider it in connection with the theory of aggression in *The Anatomy of Human Destructiveness*, published in 1973. Whereas the marketing character has been recognized and discussed in similar terms by other writers, necrophilia encountered resistance in many forms and has remained largely unexplored to the present day. Nonetheless, it represents Fromm's second most important contribution, next to the development of analytic social psychology. All three orientations of the social character—authoritarian, marketing, and necrophilous (more are described in *Man for Himself*)—gain or lose in significance, depending on social and economic circumstances. However, the current attraction of death, which is so typical of the necrophilous character, has a far different historical significance, for the existence of the nuclear threat means that the survival of the human race will depend on the strength of this attraction.

5

The Authoritarian Character

Although the character of persons in whom sadomasochistic drives are dominant can be characterized as sadomasochistic, such persons are not necessarily neurotic. It depends to a large extent on the particular tasks people have to fulfill in their social situation and what patterns of feelings and behavior are present in their culture whether or not a particular kind of character structure is "neurotic" or "normal." As a matter of fact, for great parts of the lower middle class in Germany and other European countries, the sadomasochistic character is typical, and it is this kind of character structure to which Nazi ideology had its strongest appeal. Since the term *sadomasochistic* is associated with ideas of perversion and neurosis, I prefer to speak of the sadomasochistic character, especially when not the neurotic but the normal person is meant, as the *authoritarian character*. This terminology is justifiable because the sadomasochistic person is always characterized by his attitude toward authority. He admires authority and tends to submit to it, but at the same time he wants to be an authority himself and have others submit to him. There is an additional reason for choosing this term. The Fascist system calls itself authoritarian because of the dominant role of authority in its social and political structure. By the term *authoritarian character*, we imply that it represents the personality structure which is the human basis of Fascism.

Before going on with the discussion of the authoritarian character, the term *authority* needs some clarification. Authority is not a quality one person "has," in the sense that he has property or physical qualities. Authority refers to an interpersonal relation in which one person looks upon another as somebody superior to him. But there is a fundamental difference between a kind of superiority-inferiority relation which can be called rational authority and one which may be described as inhibiting authority.

An example will show what I have in mind. The relationship between teacher and student and that between slave owner and slave are both based on the superiority of the one over the other. The interests of teacher and pupil lie in the same direction. The teacher is satisfied if he succeeds in furthering the pupil; if he has failed to do so, the failure is his and the pupil's. The slave owner, on the other hand, wants to exploit the slave as much as possible; the more he gets out of him, the more he is satisfied. At the same time, the slave seeks to defend as best he can his claims for a minimum of happiness. These interests are definitely antagonistic, as what is of advantage to the one is detrimental to the other. The superiority has a different function in both cases: In the first, it is the condition for the helping of the person subjected to the authority; in the second, it is the condition for his exploitation.

The dynamics of authority in these two types are different too: The more the student learns, the less wide is the gap between him and the teacher. He becomes more and more like the teacher himself. In other words, the authority relationship tends to dissolve itself. But when the superiority serves as a basis for exploitation, the distance becomes intensified through its long duration.

The psychological situation is different in each of these authority situations. In the first, elements of love, admiration, or gratitude are prevalent. The authority is at the same time an example with which one wants to identify one's self partially or totally. In the second situation, resentment or hostility will arise against the exploiter, subordination to whom is against one's own interests. But often, as in the case of a slave, this hatred would only lead to conflicts which would subject the slave to suffering without a chance of winning. Therefore, the tendency will usually be to repress the feeling of hatred and sometimes even to replace it by a feeling of blind admiration. This has two functions: (1) to remove the painful and dangerous feeling of hatred, and (2) to soften the feeling of humiliation. If the person who rules over me is so wonderful or perfect, then I should not be ashamed of obeying him. I cannot be his equal because he is so much stronger, wiser, better, and so on, than I am. As a result, in the inhibiting kind of authority, the element either of hatred or of irrational overestimation and admiration of the authority will tend to increase. In the rational kind of authority, it will tend to decrease in direct proportion to the degree in which the person subjected to the authority becomes stronger and thereby more similar to the authority.

The difference between rational and inhibiting authority is only a relative one. Even in the relationship between slave and master there are elements of advantage for the slave. He gets a minimum of food and protection, which at least enables him to work for his master. On the other hand, it is only in an ideal relationship between teacher and student that we find a complete lack of antagonism of interests. There are many gradations between these two extreme cases, as in the relationship of a factory worker with his boss, or a farmer's son with his father, or a hausfrau with her husband. Nevertheless, although in reality two types of authority are blended, they are essentially different, and an analysis of a concrete authority situation must always determine the specific weight of each kind of authority.

Authority does not have to be a person or institution which says: You have to do this, or you are not allowed to do that. While this kind of authority may be called external authority, authority can appear as internal authority, under the name of duty, conscience, or superego. As a matter of fact, the development of modern thinking from Protestantism to Kant's philosophy can be characterized as the substitution of internalized authority for an external one. With the political victories of the rising middle class, external authority lost prestige and man's own conscience assumed the place which external authority once had held. This change appeared to many as the victory of freedom. To submit to orders from the outside (at least in spiritual matters) appeared to be unworthy of a free man; but the conquest of his natural inclinations, and the establishment of the domination of one part of the individual, his nature, by another, his reason, will, or conscience, seemed to be the very essence of freedom. Analysis shows that conscience rules with a harshness as great as external authorities, and furthermore that frequently the contents of the orders issued by man's conscience are ultimately not governed by demands of the individual self but by social demands which have assumed the dignity of ethical norms. The rulership of conscience can be even harsher than that of external authorities, since the individual feels its orders to be his own; how can he rebel against himself?

In recent decades "conscience" has lost much of its significance. It seems as though neither external nor internal authorities play any prominent role in the individual's life. Everybody is completely "free," if only he does not interfere with other people's legitimate claims. But what we find is rather that instead of disappearing, authority has made itself invisible. Instead of overt authority, *"anonymous" authority* reigns. It is disguised as common sense, science, psychic health, normality, public opinion. It does not demand anything except the self-evident. It seems to use no pressure but only mild persuasion. Whether a mother says to her daughter, "I know you will not like to go out with that boy," or an advertisement suggests, "Smoke this brand of cigarettes—you will like their coolness," it is the same atmosphere of subtle suggestion which actually pervades our whole social life. Anonymous authority is more effective than overt authority, since one never suspects that there is any order which one is expected to follow. In external authority it is clear that there is an order and who gives it; one can fight against the authority, and in this fight personal independence and moral courage can develop. But whereas in internalized authority the command, though an internal one, remains visible, in anonymous authority both command and commander have become invisible. It is like being fired at by an invisible enemy. There is nobody and nothing to fight back against.

Returning now to the discussion of the authoritarian character, the most important feature to be mentioned is its attitude toward power. For the authoritarian character there exist, so to speak, two sexes: the powerful ones and the powerless ones. His love, admiration, and readiness for submission are automatically aroused by power, whether of a person or of an institution. Power fascinates him not for any values for which a specific power may stand, but just because it is power. Just as his "love" is automatically aroused by power, so powerless people or institutions automatically arouse his contempt. The very sight of a powerless person makes him want to attack, dominate, humiliate him. Whereas a different kind of character is appalled by the idea of attacking one who is helpless, the authoritarian character feels the more aroused the more helpless his object has become.

There is one feature of the authoritarian character which has misled many observers: a tendency to defy authority and to resent any kind of influence from "above." Sometimes this defiance overshadows the whole picture and the submissive tendencies are in the background. This type of person will constantly rebel against any kind of authority, even one that actually furthers his interests and has no elements of suppression. Sometimes the attitude toward authority is divided. Such persons might fight against one set of authorities, especially if they are disappointed by its lack of power, and at the same time or later on submit to another set of authorities which through greater power or greater promises seems to fulfill their masochistic longings. Finally, there is a type in which the rebellious tendencies are completely repressed and come to the surface only when conscious control is weakened; or they can be recognized ex posteriori, in the hatred that arises against an authority when its power is weakened and when it begins to totter. In persons of the first type in whom the rebellious attitude is in the center of the picture, one is easily led to believe that their character structure is just the opposite to that of the submissive masochistic type. It appears as if they are persons who oppose every authority on the basis of an extreme degree of independence. They look like persons who, on the basis of their inner strength and integrity, fight those forces that block their freedom and independence. However, the authoritarian character's fight against authority is essentially defiance. It is an attempt to assert himself and to overcome his own feeling of powerlessness by fighting authority, although the longing for submission remains present, whether consciously or unconsciously. The authoritarian character is never a "revolutionary"; I should like to call him a "rebel." There are many individuals and political movements that are puzzling to the superficial observer because of what seems to be an inexplicable change from "radicalism" to extreme authoritarianism. Psychologically, those people are the typical "rebels."

The attitude of the authoritarian character toward life, his whole philosophy, is determined by his emotional strivings. The authoritarian character loves those conditions that limit human freedom, he loves being submitted to fate. It depends on his social position what "fate" means to him. For a soldier it may mean the will or whim of his superior, to which he gladly submits. For the small businessman the economic laws are his fate. Crisis and prosperity to him are not social phenomena which might be changed by human activity but the expression of a higher power to which one has to submit. For those on the top of the pyramid it is basically no different. The difference lies only in the size and generality of the power to which one submits, not in the feeling of dependence as such.

Not only the forces that determine one's own life directly but also those that seem to determine life in general are felt as unchangeable fate. It is fate that there are wars and that one part of mankind has to be ruled by another. It is fate that the amount of suffering can never be less than it always has been. Fate may be rationalized philosophically as "natural law" or as "destiny of man," religiously as the "will of the Lord," ethically as "duty"—for the authoritarian character it is always a higher power outside of the individual, toward which the individual can do nothing but submit. The authoritarian character worships the past. What has been, will eternally be. To wish or to work for something that has not yet been before is crime or madness. The miracle of creation—and creation is always a miracle—is outside of his range of emotional experience. [. . .]

The courage of the authoritarian character is essentially a courage to suffer what fate or its personal representative or "leader" may have destined him for. To suffer without complaining is his highest virtue—not the courage of trying to end suffering or at least to diminish it. Not to change fate, but to submit to it, is the heroism of the authoritarian character.

He has belief in authority as long as it is strong and commanding. His belief is rooted ultimately in his doubts and constitutes an attempt to compensate them. But he has no faith, if we mean by faith the secure confidence in the realization of what now exists only as a potentiality. Authoritarian philosophy is essentially relativistic and nihilistic, in spite of the fact that it often claims so violently to have conquered relativism and in spite of its show of activity. It is rooted in extreme desperation, in the complete lack of faith, and it leads to nihilism, to the denial of life.

6

The Marketing Orientation

The marketing orientation developed as a dominant one only in the modern era. In order to understand its nature one must consider the economic function of the market in modern society as being not only analogous to this character orientation but as the basis and the main condition for its development in modern man.

Barter is one of the oldest economic mechanisms. The traditional local market, however, is essentially different from the market as it has developed in modern capitalism. Bartering on a local market offered an opportunity to meet for the purpose of exchanging commodities. Producers and customers became acquainted; they were relatively small groups; the demand was more or less known, so that the producer could produce for this specific demand.

The modern market is no longer a meeting place but a mechanism characterized by abstract and impersonal demand.[1] One produces for this market, not for a known circle of customers; its verdict is based on laws of supply and demand; and it determines whether the commodity can be sold and at what price. No matter what the *use value* of a pair of shoes may be, for instance, if the supply is greater than the demand, some shoes will be sentenced to economic death; they might as well not have been produced at all. The market day is the "day of judgment" as far as the *exchange value* of commodities is concerned.

The reader may object that this description of the market is oversimplified. The producer does try to judge the demand in advance, and under monopoly conditions even obtains a certain degree of control over it. Nevertheless, the regulatory function of the market has been, and still is, predominant enough to have a profound influence on the character

1. Cf. K. Polanyi, *The Great Transformation* (New York: Rinehart & Co., 1944).

formation of the urban middle class and, through the latter's social and cultural influence, on the whole population. The market concept of value, the emphasis on exchange value rather than on use value, has led to a similar concept of value with regard to people and particularly to oneself. The character orientation which is rooted in the experience of oneself as a commodity and of one's value as exchange value I call the marketing orientation.

In our time the marketing orientation has been growing rapidly, together with the development of a new market that is a phenomenon of the last decades—the "personality market." Clerks and salesmen, business executives and doctors, lawyers and artists all appear on this market. It is true that their legal status and economic positions are different: Some are independent, charging for their services; others are employed, receiving salaries. But all are dependent for their material success on a personal acceptance by those who need their services or who employ them.

The principle of evaluation is the same on both the personality and the commodity market: On the one, personalities are offered for sale; on the other, commodities. Value in both cases is their exchange value, for which use value is a necessary but not a sufficient condition. It is true, our economic system could not function if people were not skilled in the particular work they have to perform and were gifted only with a pleasant personality. Even the best bedside manner and the most beautifully equipped office on Park Avenue would not make a New York doctor successful if he did not have a minimum of medical knowledge and skill. Even the most winning personality would not prevent a secretary from losing her job unless she could type reasonably fast. However, if we ask what the respective weight of skill and personality as a condition for success is, we find that only in exceptional cases is success predominantly the result of skill and of certain other human qualities like honesty, decency, and integrity. Although the proportion between skill and human qualities on the one hand and "personality" on the other hand as prerequisites for success varies, the "personality factor" always plays a decisive role. Success depends largely on how well a person sells himself on the market, how well he gets his personality across, how nice a "package" he is; whether he is "cheerful," "sound," "aggressive," "reliable," "ambitious"; furthermore what his family background is, what clubs he belongs to, and whether he knows the right people. The type of personality required depends to some degree on the special field in which a person works. A stockbroker, a salesman, a secretary, a railroad executive, a college professor, or a hotel manager must each offer different kinds of personality that, regardless of their differences, must fulfill one condition: to be in demand.

The fact that in order to have success it is not sufficient to have the skill and equipment for performing a given task but that one must be able to "put across" one's personality in competition with many others shapes the attitude toward oneself. If it were enough for the purpose of making a living to rely on what one knows and what one can do, one's self-esteem would be in proportion to one's capacities, that is, to one's use value; but since success depends largely on how one sells one's personality, one experiences oneself as a commodity or rather simultaneously as the seller *and* the commodity to be sold. A person is not concerned with his life and happiness, but with becoming salable. This feeling might be compared to that of a commodity, of handbags on a counter, for instance, could they feel and think. Each handbag would try to make itself as "attractive" as possible in order to attract customers and to look as expensive as possible in order to obtain a higher price than its rivals. The handbag sold for the highest price would feel elated, since that would mean it was the most "valuable" one; the one which was not sold would feel sad and convinced of its own worthlessness. This fate might befall a bag which, though excellent in appearance and usefulness, had the bad luck to be out of date because of a change in fashion.

Like the handbag, one has to be in fashion on the personality market, and in order to be in fashion one has to know what kind of personality is most in demand. This knowledge is transmitted in a general way throughout the whole process of education, from kindergarten to college, and implemented by the family. The knowledge acquired at this early stage is not sufficient, however; it emphasizes only certain general qualities like adaptability, ambition, and sensitivity to the changing expectations of other people. The more specific picture of the models for success one gets elsewhere. The pictorial magazines, newspapers, and newsreels show the pictures and life stories of the successful in many variations. Pictorial advertising has a similar function. The successful executive who is pictured in a tailor's advertisement is the image of how one should look and be, if one is to draw down the "big money" on the contemporary personality market.

The most important means of transmitting the desired personality pattern to the average man is the motion picture. The young girl tries to emulate the facial expression, coiffure, gestures of a high-priced star as the most promising way to success. The young man tries to look and be like the model he sees on the screen. While the average citizen has little contact with the life of the most successful people, his relationship with the motion-picture stars is different. It is true that he has no real contact with them either, but he can see them on the screen again and again, can write them and receive their autographed pictures. In contrast to the time when the actor was socially despised but was nevertheless the transmitter of the works of great poets to his audience, our motion-picture stars have no great works or ideas to transmit, but their function is to serve as the link an average person has with the world of the "great." Even if he cannot hope to become as successful as they are, he can try to emulate them; they are his saints and because of their success they embody the norms for living.

Since modern man experiences himself both as the seller and as the commodity to be sold on the market, his self-esteem depends on conditions beyond his control. If he is "successful," he is valuable; if he is not, he is worthless. The degree of insecurity which results from this orientation can hardly be overestimated. If one feels that one's own value is not constituted primarily by the human qualities one possesses, but by one's success on a competitive market with ever-changing conditions, one's self-esteem is bound to be shaky and in constant need of confirmation by others. Hence one is driven to strive relentlessly for success, and any setback is a severe threat to one's self-esteem; helplessness, insecurity, and inferiority feelings are the result. If the vicissitudes of the market are the judges of one's value, the sense of dignity and pride is destroyed.

But the problem is not only that of self-evaluation and self-esteem but of one's experience of oneself as an independent entity, of one's *identity with oneself*. As we shall see later, the mature and productive individual derives his feeling of identity from the experience of himself as the agent who is one with his powers; this feeling of self can be briefly expressed as meaning *"I am what I do."* In the marketing orientation man encounters his own powers as commodities alienated from him. He is not one with them but they are masked from him because what matters is not his self-realization in the process of using them but his success in the process of selling them. Both his powers and what they create become estranged, something different from himself, something for others to judge and to use; thus his feeling of identity becomes as shaky as his self-esteem; it is constituted by the sum total of roles one can play: *"I am as you desire me."*

Ibsen has expressed this state of selfhood in Peer Gynt: Peer Gynt tries to discover his self and he finds that he is like an onion—one layer after the other can be peeled off and there is no core to be found. Since man cannot live doubting his identity, he must, in the marketing orientation, find the conviction of identity not in reference to himself and his powers but in the opinion of others about him. His prestige, status, success, the fact that he is known to others as being a certain person are a substitute for the genuine feeling of identity. This situation makes him utterly dependent on the way others look at him and forces him to keep up the role in which he once had become successful. If I and my powers are separated from each other then, indeed, is my self constituted by the price I fetch.

The way one experiences others is not different from the way one experiences oneself. Others are experienced as commodities like oneself; they too do not present *themselves* but their salable part. The difference between people is reduced to a merely quantitative difference of being *more or less* successful, attractive, hence valuable. This process is no different from what happens to commodities on the market. A painting and a pair of shoes can both be expressed in, and reduced to, their exchange value, their price; so many pairs of shoes are "equal" to one painting. In the same way the difference between people is reduced to a common element, their price on the market. Their individuality, that which is peculiar and unique in them, is valueless and, in fact, a ballast. The meaning which the word *peculiar* has assumed is quite expressive of this attitude. Instead of denoting the greatest achievement of man—that of having developed his individuality—it has become almost synonymous with *queer*. The word *equality* has also changed its meaning. The idea that all men are created equal implied that all men have the same fundamental right to be considered as ends in themselves and not as means. Today, equality has become equivalent to *interchangeability*, and is the very negation of individuality. Equality, instead of being the condition for the development of each man's peculiarity, means the extinction of individuality, the "selflessness" characteristic of the marketing orientation. Equality was conjunctive with difference, but it has become synonymous with "in-difference" and, indeed, indifference is what characterizes modern man's relationship to himself and to others.

These conditions necessarily color all human relationships. When the individual self is neglected, the relationships between people must of necessity become superficial, because not they themselves but interchangeable commodities are related. People are not able and cannot afford to be concerned with that which is unique and "peculiar" in each other. However, the market creates a kind of comradeship of its own. Everybody is involved in the same battle of competition, shares the same striving for success; all meet under the same conditions of the market (or at least believe they do). Everyone knows how the others feel because each is in the same boat: alone, afraid to fail, eager to please; no quarter is given or expected in this battle.

The superficial character of human relationships leads many to hope that they can find depth and intensity of feeling in individual love. But love for one person and love for one's neighbor are indivisible; in any given culture, love relationships are only a more intense expression of the relatedness to man prevalent in that culture. Hence it is an illusion to expect that the loneliness of man rooted in the marketing orientation can be cured by individual love.

Thinking as well as feeling is determined by the marketing orientation. Thinking assumes the function of grasping things quickly so as to be able to manipulate them successfully. Furthered by widespread and efficient education, this leads to a high degree of intelligence, but not of reason. For manipulative purposes, all that is necessary to know is the surface features of things, the superficial. The truth, to be uncovered by penetrating to the essence of phenomena, becomes an obsolete concept—truth not only in the prescientific sense of "absolute" truth, dogmatically maintained without reference to empirical data, but also in the sense of truth attained by man's reason applied to his observations and open to revisions. Most intelligence tests are attuned to this kind of thinking; they measure not so much the capacity for reason and understanding as the capacity for quick mental adaptation to a given situation; "mental adjustment tests" would be the adequate name for them.[2] For this kind of thinking the application of the categories of comparison and of quantitative measurement—rather than a thorough analysis of a given phenomenon and its quality—is essential. All problems are equally "interesting" and there is little sense of the respective differences in their importance. Knowledge itself becomes a commodity. Here, too, man is alienated from his own power; thinking and knowing are experienced as a tool to produce results. Knowledge of man himself, psychology, which in the great tradition of Western thought was held to be the condition for virtue, for right living, for happiness, has degenerated into an instrument to be used for better manipulation of others and oneself, in market research, in political propaganda, in advertising, and so on.

Evidently this type of thinking has a profound effect on our educational system. From grade school to graduate school, the aim of learning is to gather as much information as possible that is mainly useful for the purposes of the market. Students are supposed to learn so many things that they have hardly time and energy left to *think*. Not the interest in the subjects taught or in knowledge and insight as such, but the enhanced exchange value knowledge gives is the main incentive for wanting more and better education. We find today a tremendous enthusiasm for knowledge and education, but at the same time a skeptical or contemptuous

2. Cf. Ernest Schachtel, "Zum Begriff und zur Diagnosis der Persönlichkeit in ʾPersonality Testsʾ [On the concept and diagnosis of personality tests]," *Zeitschrift für Sozialforschung* (Jahrgang 6, 1937): 597–624.

attitude toward the allegedly impractical and useless thinking which is concerned "only" with the truth and which has no exchange value on the market.

Although I have presented the marketing orientation as one of the nonproductive orientations, it is in many ways so different that it belongs in a category of its own. The receptive, exploitative, and hoarding orientations have one thing in common: Each is one form of human relatedness which, if dominant in a person, is specific of him and characterizes him. [. . .] The marketing orientation, however, does not develop something which is potentially in the person (unless we make the absurd assertion that "nothing" is also part of the human equipment); its very nature is that no specific and permanent kind of relatedness is developed, but that the very changeability of attitudes is the only permanent quality of such orientation. In this orientation, those qualities are developed which can best be sold. No one particular attitude is predominant, but the emptiness which can be filled most quickly with the desired quality. This quality, however, ceases to be one in the proper sense of the word; it is only a role, the pretense of a quality, to be readily exchanged if another one is more desirable. Thus, for instance, respectability is sometimes desirable. The salesmen in certain branches of business ought to impress the public with those qualities of reliability, soberness, and respectability which were genuine in many a businessman of the nineteenth century. Now one looks for a man who instills confidence because he *looks* as if he had these qualities; what this man sells on the personality market is his ability to look the part; what kind of person is behind that role does not matter and is nobody's concern. He himself is not interested in his honesty, but in what it gets for him on the market. The premise of the marketing orientation is emptiness, the lack of any specific quality which could not be subject to change, since any persistent trait of character might conflict some day with the requirements of the market. Some roles would not fit in with the peculiarities of the person; therefore we must do away with them—not with the roles but with the peculiarities. The marketing personality must be free, free of all individuality.

7

The Necrophilous Character

I adopted the term *necrophilia* from Unamuno and have been studying the phenomenon of character-rooted necrophilia since about 1961. My theoretical concepts were gained mainly by observation of persons in analysis. The study of certain historical personalities—Hitler, for example—and the observation of individuals and of the character and behavior of social classes offered additional data for the analysis of the necrophilious character. But as much as my clinical observations influenced me, I believe the decisive impulse came from Freud's theory of the life and the death instincts. I had been deeply impressed by his concept that the striving for life and the striving for destruction were the two most fundamental forces within man; but I could not reconcile myself to Freud's theoretical explanation. Yet Freud's idea guided me to see clinical data in a new light and to reformulate—and thus to preserve—Freud's concept on a different theoretical basis and based on clinical data which, as I shall show later, link up with Freud's earlier findings on the anal character.

Necrophilia in the characterological sense can be described as *the passionate attraction to all that is dead, decayed, putrid, sickly; it is the passion to transform that which is alive into something unalive; to destroy for the sake of destruction; the exclusive interest in all that is purely mechanical. It is the passion "to tear apart living structures."*

This general description needs to be supplemented by a detailed description of various aspects of the necrophilous character.

The attraction to what is dead and putrid can be observed most clearly in the dreams of necrophilous persons:

> I find myself sitting on the toilet; I have diarrhea and defecate with an explosive force which sounds as if a bomb had exploded and the house might collapse. I want to take a bath, but when I try to turn on the

water I discover that the tub is already filled with dirty water; I see feces together with a cut-off leg and arm floating in the water.

The dreamer was an intensely necrophilous person who had had a number of similar dreams. When the analyst asked the dreamer what his feelings were in the dream about what was going on, he reported that he did not feel the situation to be frightening, but that it embarrassed him to tell the dream to the analyst.

This dream shows several elements characteristic of necrophilia, among which the theme of dismembered parts of the body is the most obvious. In addition, there is the close connection between necrophilia and anality (to be discussed later) and the theme of destruction; if we translate from symbolic to clear language, the dreamer feels that he wants to destroy the whole building by the force of his elimination. [...]

Another manifestation of the necrophilous character is the conviction that the only way to solve a problem or a conflict is by force and violence. The question involved is not whether force should be used under certain circumstances; what is characteristic for the necrophile is that force—as Simone Weil said, "the power to transform a man into a corpse"—is the first and last solution for everything; that the Gordian knot must always be cut and never dissolved patiently. Basically, these persons' answer to life's problems is destruction, never sympathetic effort, construction, or example. Theirs is the queen's answer in *Alice in Wonderland*: "Off with their heads!" Motivated by this impulse they usually fail to see other options that require no destruction, nor do they recognize how futile force has often proved to be in the long run. We find the classic expression for this attitude in King Solomon's judgment in the case of the two women who both claimed a child as her own. When the king proposes to divide the child, the true mother prefers to allow the other woman to have it; the woman who pretends to be the mother chooses to divide the child. Her solution is the typical decision of a necrophilous, property-obsessed person.

A somewhat less drastic expression of necrophilia is a marked interest in sickness in all its forms, as well as in death. An example is the mother who is always interested in her child's sicknesses, his failures, and makes dark prognoses for the future; at the same time she is unimpressed by a favorable change, she does not respond to the child's joy or enthusiasm, and she will not notice anything new that is growing within him. She does not harm the child in any obvious way, yet she may slowly strangle his joy of life, his faith in growth, and eventually she will infect him with her own necrophilous orientation.

Anyone who has occasion to listen to conversations of people of all social classes from middle age onward will be impressed by the extent of their talk about the sicknesses and death of other people. To be sure, there are a number of factors responsible for this. For many people, especially those with no outside interests, sickness and death are the only dramatic elements in their lives; it is one of the few subjects about which they can talk, aside from events in the family. But granting all this, there are many persons for whom these explanations do not suffice. They can usually be recognized by the animation and excitement that comes over them when they talk about sickness or other sad events like death, financial troubles, and so forth. The necrophilous person's particular interest in the dead is often shown not only in his conversation but in the way he reads the newspapers. He is most interested—and hence reads *first*—the death notices and obituaries; he also likes to talk about death from various aspects: what people died of, under what conditions, who died recently, who is likely to die, and so on. He likes to go to funeral parlors and cemeteries and usually does not miss an occasion to do so when it is socially opportune. It is easy to see that this affinity for burials and cemeteries is only a somewhat attenuated form of the more gross manifest interest in morgues and graves.

A somewhat less easily identifiable trait of the necrophilous person is the particular kind of lifelessness in his conversation. This is not a matter of what the conversation is about. A very intelligent, erudite necrophilous person may talk about things that would be very interesting were it not for the way in which he presents his ideas. He remains stiff, cold, aloof; his presentation of the subject is pedantic and lifeless. On the other hand, the opposite character type, the life-loving person, may talk of an experience that in itself is not particularly interesting, but there is life in the way he presents it; he is stimulating; that is why one listens with interest and pleasure. The necrophilous person is a wet blanket and a joy killer in a group; he is boring rather than animating; he deadens everything and makes people feel tired, in contrast to the biophilous person who makes people feel more alive.

Still another dimension of necrophilous reactions is the attitude toward the past and property. For the necrophilous character only the past is experienced as quite real, not the present or the future. What has been, i.e., what is dead, rules his life: institutions, laws, property, traditions, and possessions. Briefly, *things rule man; having* rules *being; the dead* rule *the living*. In the necrophile's thinking—personal, philosophical, and political—the past is sacred, nothing new is valuable, drastic change is a crime against the "natural" order.

Another aspect of necrophilia is the relation to color. The necrophilous person generally has a predilection for dark, light-absorbing colors, such as black or brown, and a dislike for bright, radiant colors. One can observe this preference in their dress or in the colors they choose if they paint. Of course, in cases when dark clothes are worn out of tradition, the color has no significance in relation to character. [...]

The language of the necrophilous person is characterized by the predominant use of words referring to destruction and to feces and toilets. While the use of the word "shit" has become very widespread today, it is nevertheless not difficult to discern people whose favorite word it is, far beyond its current frequency. An example is a twenty-two-year-old man for whom everything was "shitty": life, people, ideas, and nature. The same young man said proudly of himself: "I am an artist of destruction." [...]

Lewis Mumford (1967) has shown the connection between destructiveness and power-centered "megamachines" as they existed in Mesopotamia and Egypt some five thousand years ago, societies that have, as he has pointed out, much in common with the megamachines of Europe and North America today.

Let us begin with the consideration of the simplest and most obvious characteristics of contemporary industrial man: the stifling of his focal interest in people, nature, and living structures, together with the increasing attraction of mechanical, nonalive artifacts. Examples abound. All over the industrialized world there are men who feel more tender toward, and are more interested in, their automobiles than their wives. They are proud of their car; they cherish it; they wash it (even many of those who could pay to have this job done), and in some countries many give it a loving nickname; they observe it and are concerned at the slightest symptom of a dysfunction. To be sure a car is not a sexual object—but it is an object of love; life without a car seems to some more intolerable than life without a woman. Is this attachment to automobiles not somewhat peculiar, or even perverse?

Or another example, taking pictures. Anyone who has the occasion to observe tourists—or maybe to observe himself—can discover that taking pictures has become a substitute for seeing. Of course, you have to look in order to direct your lens to the desired object; then you push the button, the film is processed and taken home. But *looking* is not *seeing*. Seeing is a human function, one of the greatest gifts with which man is endowed; it requires activity, inner openness, interest, patience, concentration. Taking a *snapshot* (the aggressive expression is significant) means essentially to transform the act of seeing into an object—the picture to be shown later to friends as a proof that "you have been there." The same is the case with those music lovers for whom listening to music is only the pretext for experimenting with the technical qualities of their record players or high-fidelity sets and the particular technical improvements they have added. Listening to music has been transformed for them into studying the product of high technical performance.

Another example is the gadgeteer, the person who is intent on replacing every application of human effort with a "handy," "work-saving" contraption. Among such people may be numbered the sales personnel who make even the simplest addition by machine, as well as people who refuse to walk even a block, but will automatically take the car. And most of us probably know of home-workshop gadgetmakers who construct mechanically operated devices that by the mere press of a button or flick of a switch can start a fountain, or swing open a door, or set off even more impractical, often absurd, Rube Goldberg contrivances.

It should be clear that in speaking of this kind of behavior I do not imply that using an automobile, or taking pictures, or using gadgets is in itself a manifestation of necrophilous tendencies. But it assumes this quality when it becomes a *substitute* for interest in life and for exercising the rich functions with which the human being is endowed. I also do not imply that the engineer who is passionately interested in the construction of machines of all kinds shows, for this reason, a necrophilous tendency. He may be a very productive person with great love of life that he expresses in his attitude toward people, toward nature, toward art, and in his constructive technical ideas. I am referring, rather, to those individuals whose interest in artifacts has *replaced* their interest in what is alive and who deal with technical matters in a pedantic and unalive way. [. . .]

Is necrophilia really characteristic for man in the second half of the twentieth century in the United States and in other equally highly developed capitalist or state capitalist societies?

This new type of man, after all, is not interested in feces or corpses; in fact, he is so phobic toward corpses that he makes them look more alive than the person was when living. (This does not seem to be a reaction formation, but rather a part of the whole orientation that denies natural, not man-made reality.) But he does something much more drastic. He turns his interest away from life, persons, nature, ideas—in short from everything that is alive; he transforms all life into things, including himself and the manifestations of his human faculties of reason, seeing, hearing, tasting, loving. Sexuality becomes a technical skill (the "love machine"); feelings are flattened and sometimes substituted for by sentimentality; joy, the expression of intense aliveness, is replaced by "fun" or excitement;

and whatever love and tenderness man has is directed toward machines and gadgets. The world becomes a sum of lifeless artifacts; from synthetic food to synthetic organs, the whole man becomes part of the total machinery that he controls and is simultaneously controlled by. He has no plan, no goal for life, except doing what the logic of technique determines him to do. He aspires to make robots as one of the greatest achievements of his technical mind, and some specialists assure us that the robot will hardly be distinguished from living men. This achievement will not seem so astonishing when man himself is hardly distinguishable from a robot.

The world of life has become a world of "no-life"; persons have become "nonpersons," a world of death. Death is no longer symbolically expressed by unpleasant-smelling feces or corpses. Its symbols are now clean, shining machines; men are not attracted to smelly toilets, but to structures of aluminum and glass. But the reality behind this antiseptic facade becomes increasingly visible. Man, in the name of progress, is transforming the world into a stinking and poisonous place (and this is *not* symbolic). He pollutes the air, the water, the soil, the animals—and himself. He is doing this to a degree that has made it doubtful whether the earth will still be livable within a hundred years from now. He knows the facts, but in spite of many protesters, those in charge go on in the pursuit of technical "progress" and are willing to sacrifice all life in the worship of their idol. In earlier times men also sacrificed their children or war prisoners, but never before in history has man been willing to sacrifice all life to the Moloch—his own and that of all his descendents. It makes little difference whether he does it intentionally or not. If he had no knowledge of the possible danger, he might be acquitted from responsibility. But it is the necrophilous element in his character that prevents him from making use of the knowledge he has.

The same is true for the preparation of nuclear war. The two superpowers are constantly increasing their capacities to destroy each other, and at least large parts of the human race with them. Yet they have not done anything serious to eliminate the danger—and the only serious thing would be the destruction of all nuclear weapons. In fact, those in charge were already close to using nuclear weapons several times—and gambled with the danger. Strategic reasoning—for instance. Herman Kahn's *On Thermonuclear War* (1960)—calmly raises the question whether fifty million dead would still be "acceptable." That this is the spirit of necrophilia can hardly be questioned.

The phenomena about which there is so much indignation—drug addiction, crime, the cultural and spiritual decay, contempt for genuine ethical values—are all related to the growing attraction to death and dirt. How can one expect that the young, the poor, and those without hope would not be attracted to decay when it is promoted by those who direct the course of modern society? [. . .]

To conclude this discussion of necrophilia, it may be helpful to present a brief sketch of the relation of this concept to Freud's concept of the death instinct and the life instinct (Eros). It is the effort of Eros to combine organic substance into ever larger unities, whereas the death instinct tries to separate and to disintegrate living structure. The relation of the death instinct with necrophilia hardly needs any further explanation. In order to elucidate the relation between life instinct and biophilia, however, a short explanation of the latter is necessary.

Biophilia is the passionate love of life and of all that is alive; it is the wish to further growth, whether in a person, a plant, an idea, or a social group. The biophilous person prefers to construct rather than to retain. He is capable of wondering, and he prefers to see something new rather than to find confirmation of the old. He loves the adventure of living more than he does certainty. He sees the whole rather than only the parts, structures rather than summations. He wants to mold and to influence by love, reason, and example; not by force, by cutting things apart, by the bureaucratic manner of administering people as if they were things. Because he enjoys life and all its manifestations he is not a passionate consumer of newly packaged "excitement."

Biophilic ethics have their own principle of good and evil. Good is all that serves life; evil is all that serves death. Good is reverence for life, all that enhances life, growth, unfolding. Evil is all that stifles life, narrows it down, cuts it into pieces.

The difference between Freud's concept and the one presented here does not lie in their substance but in the fact that in Freud's concept both tendencies have equal rank, as it were, both being biologically given. Biophilia, on the other hand, is understood to refer to a biologically normal impulse, while necrophilia is understood as a *psychopathological* phenomenon. The latter necessarily emerges as the result of stunted growth, of psychical "crippledness." It is the outcome of unlived life, of the failure to arrive at a certain stage beyond narcissism and indifference. *Destructiveness is not parallel to, but the alternative to biophilia. Love of life or love of the dead is the fundamental alternative that confronts every human being. Necrophilia grows as the development of biophilia is stunted. Man is biologically endowed with the capacity for biophilia, but psychologically he has the potential for necrophilia as an alternative solution.*

The psychical necessity for the development of necrophilia as a result of crippledness must be understood in reference to man's existential situation. If man cannot create anything or move anybody, if he cannot break out of the prison of his total narcissism, he can escape the unbearable sense of vital impotence and nothingness only by affirming himself in the act of destruction of the life that he is unable to create. Great effort, patience, and care are not required; for destruction all that is necessary is strong arms, or a knife, or a gun.

I will close this discussion of necrophilia with some general clinical and methodological remarks.

1. The presence of one or two traits is insufficient for the diagnosis of a necrophilous character. This is so for various reasons. Sometimes a particular behavior that would seem to indicate necrophilia may not be a character trait but be due to cultural tradition or other similar factors.

2. On the other hand, it is not necessary to find all characteristically necrophilous features together in order to make the diagnosis. There are many factors, personal and cultural, that are responsible for this unevenness; in addition, some necrophilous traits may not be discovered in people who hide them successfully.

3. It is of particular importance to understand that only a relatively small minority are *completely* necrophilous; one might consider them as severely pathological cases and look for a genetic disposition for this illness. As is to be expected on biological grounds, the vast majority are not entirely without some, even if weak, biophilous tendencies. Among them will be a certain percentage of people whose necrophilia is so predominant that we are justified in calling them necrophilous persons. By far the larger number are those in whom necrophilous trends are to be found together with biophilous trends strong enough to create an internal conflict that is often very productive. The outcome of this conflict for the motivation of a person depends on many variables. First of all, on the respective intensity of each trend; second, on the presence of social conditions that would strengthen one of the two respective orientations; furthermore, on particular events in the life of the person that can incline him in the one or the other direction. Then come the people who are so predominantly biophilous that their necrophilous impulses are easily curbed or repressed, or serve to build up a particular sensitivity *against* the necrophilous tendencies in themselves and others. Eventually there is the group of people—again only a small minority—in whom there is no trace of necrophilia, who are pure biophiles motivated by the most intense and pure love for all that is alive. Albert Schweitzer, Albert Einstein, and Pope John XXIII are among the well-known recent examples of this minority.

Consequently there is no fixed border between the necrophilous and the biophilous orientations. As with most other character traits, there are as many combinations as there are individuals. For all practical purposes, however, it is quite possible to distinguish between predominantly necrophilous and predominantly biophilous persons.

4. Since most of the methods that can be used for discovering the necrophilous character have already been mentioned, I can be very brief in summing them up. They are: (*a*) minute observation of a person's behavior, especially what is unintended, including facial expression, choice of words, general philosophy, but also the most important decisions the person has made in his life; (*b*) study of dreams, jokes, fantasies; (*c*) evaluation of a person's treatment of others, the effect on them, and what kind of people are liked or disliked; (*d*) the use of projective tests like the Rorschach inkblot test. (M. Maccoby has used the test for the diagnosis of necrophilia with satisfactory results.)

5. It is hardly necessary to stress that severely necrophilous persons are very dangerous. They are the haters, the racists, those in favor of war, bloodshed, and destruction. They are dangerous not only if they are political leaders, but also as the potential cohorts for a dictatorial leader. They become the executioners, terrorists, torturers; without them no terror system could be set up. But the less intense necrophiles are also politically important; while they may not be among its first adherents, they are necessary for the existence of a terror regime because they form a solid basis, although not necessarily a majority, for it to gain and hold power.

6. Considering these facts, would it not be of great social and political significance to know what percentage of the population can be considered to be predominantly necrophilous or predominantly biophilous? To know not only the respective incidence of each group but also how they are related to age, sex, education, class, occupation, and geographical location? We study political opinions, value judgments, etc., and get satisfactory results for the whole American population by the use of adequate sampling techniques. But the results tell us only what *opinions* people have, not what their *character* is—in other words, what the *effective* convictions are that motivate them. If we were to study an equally adequate sample, but with a different method that would permit us to recognize the driving and largely unconscious forces behind manifest behavior and opinions, we would, indeed, know a great deal more about the intensity and direction of human energy in the United States. We might even protect ourselves from some of the surprises that, once they have happened, are declared to be unexplainable. Or is it that we are interested only in the energy that is needed for production and not in the forms of *human* energy that is in itself a decisive factor in the social process?

PART III

The Study of Mother Right and Its Significance for Social Psychology

Fromm rarely grew insistent when he recommended books to read. One exception was Bachofen: "Have you read anything by him? Read him! At least read the introduction to *Mother Right*. You will learn a lot from it." Fromm never gave a recommendation that did not spring from personal experience. What had he himself learned from Bachofen?

Societies and cultures have not only a psychic structure, i.e., a social character; they also have a "sexual orientation," in a manner of speaking, tending toward either father right or mother right. And depending on which right predominates, certain other laws of thinking, social life, and psychic development predominate as well.

Fromm had intuited some of this even before he became acquainted with the writings of Bachofen, Morgan, and Briffault in the early thirties. His doubts about the Freudian view of the Oedipus complex were increased through contact with Georg Groddeck in Baden-Baden and with Karen Horney and grew into open criticism of the patriarchal terms in which Freud's psychoanalytic theory was conceived.

There is no doubt that Fromm preferred mother-centered cultures. But there is also no doubt that Fromm took a skeptical view of feminism, since in his eyes feminism either aggressively attempts to copy male supremacy or exhausts itself in the struggle against this supremacy rather than striving for an integration of both aspects. Fromm's enthusiasm for Bachofen's insights went beyond the following description of the present-day significance of the meaning of the theory of mother right. He was fascinated by the realization that the unconditional love of the mother is far more decisive for human psychological development than the problems raised by either the Oedipus complex or penis envy. Unconditional love is also the decisive dimension for the course of psychotherapy. In spite of all his differences with psychoanalytic orthodoxy, Fromm felt that his work here related to that of analysts such as Sándor Ferenczi and Michael Balint.

8

The Significance of the Theory of Mother Right for Today

The fact that Bachofen's theories of mother right and the matriarchal societies found relatively little attention in the nineteenth century and the first half of the twentieth is sufficiently explained by the circumstance that up to the end of the First World War the patriarchal system in Europe and America had remained unshaken, so that the very idea of women as the center of a social and religious structure seemed unthinkable and absurd. By the same token, the social and psychological changes that have taken place in the last four decades should provide the reason why the problem of matriarchate should arouse new and intense interest; only now, it seems, are changes occurring which call for a new evaluation of ideas that had remained dormant for over a hundred years. Before writing about these changes, however, let me give the reader not familiar with Bachofen and Morgan a brief introduction to their view of the principles and values of matriarchal society.

According to Bachofen, the matriarchal principle is that of life, unity, and peace. The woman, in caring for the infant, extends her love beyond her own self to other human beings, and projects all her gifts and imagination to the aim of preserving and beautifying the existence of another human being. The principle of matriarchy is that of universality, while the patriarchal system is that of restrictions. The idea of the universal brotherhood of man is rooted in the principle of motherhood, but vanishes with the development of patriarchal society. Matriarchate is the basis of the principle of universal freedom and equality, of peace and tender humaneness. It is also the basis for principled concern for material welfare and worldly happiness.[1]

From *The Crisis of Psychoanalysis* by Erich Fromm. Copyright © 1970 by Erich Fromm. Reprinted by permission of Henry Holt and Company, Inc.
    1. See J. J. Bachofen, *Myth, Religion, and Mother Right*, ed. Joseph Campbell (Princeton, N.J.: Princeton University Press, 1968), 69–121.

Quite independently, L. H. Morgan[2] came to the conclusion that the kinship system of the American Indians—similar to that found in Asia, Africa, and Australia—was based on the matriarchal principle, and he asserted that the higher forms of civilization "will be a repetition, but on a higher level, of the principles of liberty, equality and fraternity which characterized the ancient gens." Even this brief presentation of these principles of matriarchate should make clear why I attach such importance to the following social-psychological changes:

1. The *failure of the patriarchal-authoritarian system* to fulfill its function; its inability to prevent large and devastating wars and terroristic dictatorships; its incapacity to act in order to prevent future catastrophes, such as nuclear-biological-chemical war, starvation in large parts of the colonial world, and the catastrophic results of increasing poisoning of air, water, and soil.

2. The *democratic revolution*, which has defeated the traditional authoritarian structures, and replaced them by democratic structures. The process of democratization has gone together with the emergence of a technological, affluent society that does not mainly require personal obedience but operates, rather, on the basis of teamwork and manipulated consent.

3. The *women's revolution*, which, although not complete, has gone a long way in carrying out the radical ideas of the Enlightenment about the equality of men and women. This revolution has dealt a severe blow to patriarchal authority in the capitalist countries as well as in a country as conservative as the Soviet Union.

4. The *children's and adolescents' revolution*: In the past, children were able to rebel only in inadequate ways—refusing to eat, crying, constipation, bed-wetting, and general obstinacy—but since the nineteenth century they have found spokesmen (Pestalozzi, Freud, and others) who stressed that children have a will and passions of their own and must be taken seriously. This trend continued with increasing force and insight in the twentieth century, and Dr. Benjamin Spock became its most influential spokesman. As far as adolescents and post-adolescents are concerned, they now speak for themselves—and no longer in a subdued voice. They demand the right to be heard, to be taken seriously, to be active subjects and not passive objects in the arrangements governing their lives. They attack patriarchal authority directly, vigorously—and sometimes viciously.

5. The *vision* of the *consumer's paradise*. Our consumer culture creates a new vision: If we continue on the path of technological progress, we

2. In his *Systems of Consanguinity and Affinity* (1871) and *Ancient Society* (1877).

shall eventually arrive at a point where no desire, not even the ever-newly created ones, remains unfulfilled; fulfillment will be instant and without the need to exert any effort. In this vision, technique assumes the characteristics of the Great Mother, a technical instead of a natural one, who nurses her children and pacifies them with a never-ceasing lullaby (in the form of radio and television). In the process, man becomes emotionally an infant, feeling secure in the hope that mother's breasts will always supply abundant milk, and that decisions need no longer be made by the individual. Instead, they are made by the technological apparatus itself, interpreted and executed by the technocrats, the new priests of an emerging matriarchal religion, with Technique as its goddess.

6. Certain matriarchal tendencies can also be observed in some sectors of the—more or less—radical youth. Not only because they are strictly anti-authoritarian; but also because of their embracing of the above-mentioned values and attitudes of the matriarchal world, as described by Bachofen and Morgan. The idea of group sex (whether in its middle-class, suburban forms or in radical communes with shared sex) has a close connection with Bachofen's description of the early matriarchal stage of mankind. The question can also be raised as to whether the tendency to diminish sexual differences in appearance, dress, etc., is not also related to the tendency to abolish the traditional status of the male, and to make the two sexes less polarized, leading to regression (emotionally) to the pregenital stage of the infant.

There are other traits which tend to support the assumption that there is an increasing matriarchal trend among this section of the young generation. The "group" itself seems to assume the function of the mother: the need for immediate satisfaction of desires; the passive-receptive attitude, which is most clearly indicated in the drug obsession; the need to huddle together and for touching each other physically—all seem to indicate a regression to the infant's tie to mother. In all these respects the young generation does not seem to be as different from their elders as they think themselves to be, although their consumption patterns have a different content and their despair is expressed overtly and aggressively. The disturbing element in this neo-matriarchalism is that it is a mere negation of patriarchalism and a straight regression to an infantile pattern, rather than a dialectical progression to a higher form of matriarchalism. H. Marcuse's appeal to the young seems to rest largely on the fact that he is the spokesman for infantile regression to matriarchalism and that he makes this principle more attractive by using revolutionary rhetoric.

7. Perhaps not unrelated to these social changes is a development in psychoanalysis that is beginning to correct Freud's older idea about the

central role of the *sexual* bond between son and mother, and the resulting hostility toward the father, with the new notion that there is an early "pre-Oedipal" intense bond between the infant and the mother, regardless of the child's sex. In *The Crisis of Psychoanalysis* (chapter 1) I indicated how this development began in Freud's later writings, and was taken up by others, although very gingerly. Bachofen's work, if thoroughly studied by psychoanalysts, will prove to be of immense value for the understanding of this nonsexual mother fixation.

I want to conclude these introductory remarks with a theoretical consideration. As the reader will see in the following chapter, the matriarchal principle is that of unconditional love, natural equality, emphasis on the bonds of blood and soil, compassion, and mercy; the patriarchal principle is that of conditional love, hierarchical structure, abstract thought, man-made laws, the state, and justice. In the last analysis, mercy and justice represent the two principles, respectively.

It seems that in the course of history the two principles have sometimes clashed with each other violently and that sometimes they formed a synthesis (for instance, in the Catholic church, or in Marx's concept of socialism). If they are opposed to each other, the matriarchal principle manifests itself in motherly overindulgence and infantilization of the child, preventing its full maturity; fatherly authority becomes harsh domination and control, based on the child's fear and feelings of guilt. This is the case in the relationship of the child to father-mother, as well as in the spirit of patriarchal and matriarchal societies which determine the family structure. The purely matriarchal society stands in the way of the full development of the individual, thus preventing technical, rational, artistic progress. The purely patriarchal society cares nothing for love and equality; it is only concerned with man-made laws, the state, abstract principles, obedience. It is beautifully described in Sophocles' *Antigone* in the person and system of Creon, the prototype of a fascist leader.

When the patriarchal and matriarchal principles form a synthesis, however, each of the two principles is colored by the other: motherly love by justice and rationality, and fatherly love by mercy and equality.

Today the fight against patriarchal authority seems to be destroying the patriarchal principle, suggesting a return to a matriarchal principle in a regressive and nondialectic way. A viable and progressive solution lies only in a new synthesis of the opposites, one in which the opposition between mercy and justice is replaced by a union of the two on a higher level.

9

The Theory of Mother Right and Social Psychology

Whatever the present status of matriarchy research, however, it seems certain that there are societal structures which can be called matricentric. And if we are to understand the social structures of the present day and their transformations, attention should be given to the present and future findings of this research.

The libidinal strivings of human beings are among the social "productive forces" in society. By virtue of their flexibility and changeability, they can adapt themselves considerably to the existing economic and social situation of the group—though there are limits to this adaptability. The psychic structure shared by the members of a social group represents an indispensable support for the maintenance of social stability. This structure, of course, is a support for stability only so long as the contradictions between the psychic structure and economic conditions do not go beyond a certain threshold; if this threshold is passed, the psychic forces tend to change or dissolve the existing order; it is important, though, to remember that the psychic structures of different classes can be radically different or even opposed to each other, depending on their function in the social process.

Although the individual is psychically different from the members of his own group, because of his individual constitution and personal life experiences—particularly those of early childhood—a large sector of his psychic structure is the product of adaptation to the situation of his class and the whole society in which he lives. Our knowledge about the factors determining the psychic structure of a given class or society, and hence about the psychic "productive forces" that are operative in a given society, is far less advanced than our knowledge about economic and social structures. One of the reasons for this is that the student of these problems is himself molded by the psychic structure typical for his society; accordingly, he comprehends only that which is like him. He easily makes the mistake of regarding his own psychic structure, or that of his society, as "human nature." He can readily overlook the fact that, under different social conditions, quite different drive structures have been and can be operative as productive forces.

The study of "matricentric" cultures is important for the social sciences. Because it brings to light psychic structures that are wholly different from those observed in our society; at the same time, it throws new light on the "patricentric" principle.

The patricentric complex is a psychic structure in which one's relationship to the father (or his psychological equivalents) is the central relationship. In his concept of the (positive) Oedipus complex, Freud uncovered one of the decisive features of this structure—although he overestimated its universality because he lacked the necessary distance from his own society. The sexual impulses of the male infant, which are directed to his mother as the first and most important female "love-object," cause him to regard his father as a rival. This constellation acquires its characteristic significance from the further fact that in the patriarchal family the father simultaneously functions as the authority who governs the child's life. Quite apart from the physiological impossibility of the fulfillment of the child's wishes, the father's dual role has another effect that Freud pointed out: The child's desire to take the place of his father leads him to identify with his father to some degree. The child introjects the father, insofar as the latter is the representative of moral dictates, and this introjection is a powerful source for the formation of conscience. But since this process is only partially successful, the child's rivalry with the father leads to the development of an ambivalent emotional attitude. On the one hand, the child wants to be loved by his father; on the other hand, he more or less openly rebels against him.

However, the patricentric complex is also shaped by the psychic processes going on in the father himself. For one thing, he is jealous of his son. This is partly due to the fact that his lifeline is on the wane by comparison with that of his son. But an even more important cause of this jealousy is socially conditioned: It stems from the fact that the child's life situation is relatively free of social obligations. It is clear that this jealousy is greater where the weight of paternal responsibilities is heavier.

Still more important in determining the father's attitude toward his son are social and economic factors. Depending on economic circumstances, the son is either the heir to his father's estate or the future provider for his father in sickness and old age. He represents a sort of capital investment. From an economic viewpoint, the sums invested in his education and professional training are quite akin to those contributed toward accident insurance and old-age pensions.

Moreover, the son plays an important role insofar as the father's social prestige is concerned. His contributions to society and the concomitant social recognition can increase his father's prestige; his social failure can diminish or even destroy his father's prestige. (An economically or socially successful marriage by the son plays an equivalent role.)

Because of the son's social and economic function, the goal of his education is ordinarily not his personal happiness—i.e., the maximum development of his own personality; it is rather his maximum usefulness in contributing to the father's economic or social needs. Frequently, therefore, we find an objective conflict between the son's happiness and his usefulness; but this conflict is usually not consciously noticed by the father, since the ideology of his society leads him to see both goals as identical. The situation is further complicated by the fact that the father frequently identifies himself with his son: He expects his son not only to be socially useful, but also to fulfill his own unsatisfied wishes and fantasies.

These social functions of the son play a decisive role in the quality of the father's love: He loves his son on the condition that the son fulfill the expectations that are centered around him. If this is not the case, the father's love can end, or even turn to disdain or hate.

The conditional nature of paternal love typically leads to two results: (1) loss of the psychic security that comes from the knowledge that one is loved unconditionally; (2) intensification of the role of conscience—i.e., the person develops an outlook in which the fulfillment of duty becomes the central concern of life, because only that can provide some minimum guarantee of being loved. But even maximal fulfillment of the demands of conscience will not prevent guilt feelings from arising, because the person's performance will always fall short of the ideals set before him.

By contrast, a mother's love for the child is typically of a wholly different character. (Obviously, I am talking here about paternal or maternal love in an ideal sense. The love of a particular father or mother will fall far short of this ideal presentation—for a wide variety of reasons.) This is due, first and foremost, to the fact that it is completely unconditional in the first few years of life. Mother's care of the helpless infant is not dependent on any moral or social obligations to be carried out by the child; there is not even an obligation to return her love. The unconditional nature of motherly love is a biological necessity which may also foster a propensity for unconditional love in the woman's emotional disposition. The certainty that mother's (or her psychological equivalent's) love is not dependent on any conditions means that the fulfillment of moral dictates plays a much smaller role, since it is not the condition for being loved.

The traits just described differ sharply from the image of the mother that is cherished in present-day patricentric society. Basically, this society only knows about courage and heroism on the part of the man (in whom these qualities are really tinged with a large dose of narcissism). The image of the mother, on the other hand, has been a distorted one of senti-mentality and weakness. In place of unconditional motherly love, which embraces not only one's own children but all children and all human beings, we find the specifically bourgeois sentiment of possessiveness in-jected into the mother image.

This change in the mother image represents a socially conditioned dis-tortion of the mother-child relationship. A further consequence of this distortion—and also an expression of the Oedipus complex—is the attitude in which the desire to be loved by the mother is replaced by the desire to protect her and place her on a pedestal. No longer does the mother have the function of protecting; now she is to be protected and kept "pure." This reaction formation (distorting the original relationship to one's mother) is also extended to other mother symbols, such as country, nation, and the soil; and it plays an important role in the extremely patricentric ide-ologies of the present day. Mother and her psychological equivalents have not disappeared in these ideologies, but they have changed their function from protecting figures to figures in need of protection.

Summing up, we can say that the patricentric individual—and society— is characterized by a complex of traits in which the following are pre-dominant: a strict superego, guilt feelings, docile love for paternal authority, desire and pleasure at dominating weaker people, acceptance of suffering as a punishment for one's own guilt, and a damaged capacity for happi-ness. The matricentric complex, by contrast, is characterized by a feeling of optimistic trust in mother's unconditional love, far fewer guilt feelings, a far weaker superego, and a greater capacity for pleasure and happiness. Along with these traits there also develops the ideal of motherly compas-sion and love for the weak and others in need of help.

While both types may well be found in any given society—depending primarily on the child's family constellation—it does seem that, as an average type, each is characteristic for a particular type of society. The patricentric type is probably dominant in bourgeois Protestant society, while the matricentric type would play a relatively major role in the Middle Ages and in southern European society today. This leads us to Weber's

treatment of the connection between bourgeois capitalism and the Protestant work ethos, in contrast to the connection between Catholicism and
the work ethos of Catholic countries.

Whatever objections may be raised against specific theses of Weber, the
fact of such a connection is now an assured part of scholarly knowledge.
Weber himself treated the problem on the conscious and ideological level.
But a complete understanding of the interrelationship can only be achieved
by an analysis of the drive that serves as the basis for bourgeois capitalism
and the Protestant spirit.

While Catholicism also exhibits many patricentric traits—God the Father, hierarchy of male priests, etc.—the important role of the matricentric
complex in it cannot be denied. The Virgin Mary and the church herself
psychologically represent the Great Mother who shelters all her children
in her bosom. Indeed, certain maternal traits are ascribed to God himself—
though not in a conscious way. The individual "son of the church" can
be sure of mother church's love, so long as he remains her child or
returns to her bosom. This child relationship is effected sacramentally. To
be sure, moral dictates play a major role. But a complicated mechanism
operates to insure that these dictates retain their necessary social weight
while, at the same time, the individual believer can have the certainty of
being loved without reference to the moral sphere. Catholicism produces
guilt feelings in no small measure; at the same time, however, it provides the means for freeing oneself from these feelings. The price one
must pay is affective attachment to the church and her servants.

Protestantism, on the other hand, has done a thorough job of expurgat-
ing the matricentric traits of Christianity. Mother substitutes, such as the
Virgin Mary or the church, have disappeared, as have maternal traits in
God. At the center of Luther's theology we find doubt or despair that
sinful man can have any certainty of being loved. And there is only one
remedy: faith. In Calvinism and many other Protestant sects, this remedy
proves to be insufficient. It is complemented in a decisive way by the role
assigned to the fulfillment of one's duty ("innerworldly asceticism"), and
by the necessity for "success" in secular life as the only proof of God's
favor and grace.

The rise of Protestantism is conditioned by the same social and economic factors that made possible the rise of the "spirit" of capitalism.
And, like every religion, Protestantism has the function of continually
reproducing and strengthening the drive structure that is necessary for a
particular society. The patricentric complex—in which fulfillment of
duty and success are the major driving forces of life, while pleasure and
happiness play a secondary role—represents one of the most powerful

productive forces behind the enormous economic and cultural efforts of capitalism. Until the capitalist era, people (e.g., slaves) had to be compelled by physical force to dedicate every ounce of energy to economically useful work. Through the influence of the patricentric complex, people began to show the same total dedication of their own "free will," because the external compunction was now internalized. The internalization was effected most completely among the ruling classes of bourgeois society, who were the authentic representatives of the specifically bourgeois work ethos. In contrast to external force, however, the internalization process led to a different result: Fulfilling the dictates of conscience offered a satisfaction that contributed greatly to the solidification of the patricentric structure.

This satisfaction, however, was quite limited, because fulfillment of duty and economic success were poor substitutes for traits now lost: the capacity to enjoy life, and the inner security derived from knowing that one is loved unconditionally. Moreover, the spirit of *homo homini lupus* led to personal isolation and an incapacity for love—a heavy psychic burden on the psyche, which tended to undermine the patricentric structure, even though the decisive factors operating to undermine the structure were rooted in economic changes.

While patricentric structure had been the psychic driving force behind the economic achievements of bourgeois Protestant society, at the same time it produced the conditions that would destroy the patricentric structure and lead to a renaissance of a matricentric one. The growth of man's productive capacity made it possible, for the first time in history, to visualize the realization of a social order that previously had only found expression in fairy tales and myths, an order where all men would be provided with the material means necessary for their real happiness, with relatively little expenditure of individual effort in actual labor, where men's energies would be expended primarily in developing their human potential rather than in creating the economic goods that are absolutely necessary for the existence of a civilization.

The most progressive philosophers of the French enlightenment outgrew the emotional and ideological complex of the patricentric structure. But the real, full-fledged representative of the new matricentric tendencies proved to be the class whose motive for total dedication to work was prompted basically by economic considerations rather than by an internalized compunction: the working class. This same emotional structure provided one of the conditions for the effective influence of Marxist socialism on the working class—insofar as its influence depended on the specific nature of their drive structure.

The psychic basis of the Marxist social program was predominantly the matricentric complex. Marxism is the idea that if the productive capabilities of the economy were organized rationally, every person would be provided with a sufficient supply of the goods he needed—no matter what his role in the production process was; furthermore, all this could be done with far less work on the part of each individual than had been necessary up to now, and finally, every human being has an unconditional right to happiness in life, and this happiness basically resides in the "harmonious unfolding of one's personality"—all these ideas were the rational, scientific expression of ideas that could only be expressed in fantasy under earlier economic conditions: Mother Earth gives all her children what they need, without regard for their merits.

It is this connection between matricentric tendencies and socialist ideas that explains why the "materialist-democratic" character of matriarchal societies led socialist authors to express such warm sympathy for the theory of matriarchy.

PART IV

A New View of Society

Erich Fromm's approach and thinking are often seen as similar to those of Carl Gustav Jung. However, Jung's doctrine of archetypes and his assumption of the existence of a collective unconscious are fundamentally different from Fromm's theory of social character and the social unconscious, particularly with regard to cultural and social determination of the unconscious. Fromm speaks of forces to which every society and culture give their own unique stamp, and whose fate—access to consciousness or repression—is also decided by each society or culture separately.

The goal of all depth psychology is to deal with the unconscious, in order to experience the *whole* human being. Society determines which parts of themselves its members are aware of and whether the progressive or regressive forces prevail. All psychotherapeutic efforts, as well as all pedagogical, educational, ethical, and religious efforts to influence and shape the whole person, have in common the goal of making unconscious forces fruitful and productive. The unconscious is always inextricably linked to society. If the forces within people that make living relationships possible—their reason and love—are not in demand, because their society requires passive consumers of goods and products instead, then society is sick and the normal becomes pathologic. Mental health and survival are possible only if economic and social conditions are altered; social theory and social criticism become the prerequisites for all psychotherapeutic endeavors.

Fromm did not begin to act on these insights until relatively late in life. In 1955 his book *The Sane Society* appeared, in which he visualizes his ideas of a humane society in the form of a humanistic socialism. Fromm became active in the peace and disarmament movements and for a time was even a member of the Socialist party in the United States. Modified versions of his proposals for altering society were published in *The Revolution of Hope: Toward a Humanized Technology* (1968) and *To Have or To Be?* (1976).

10

The Social Unconscious

The social character which makes people act and think as they have to act and think from the standpoint of the proper functioning of their society is only one link between the social structure and ideas. The other link lies in the fact that each society determines which thoughts and feelings shall be permitted to arrive at the level of awareness and which have to remain unconscious. Just as there is a social character, there is also a *social unconscious.*

By *social unconscious* I refer to those areas of repression which are common to most members of a society; these commonly repressed elements are those contents which a given society cannot permit its members to be aware of if the society with its specific contradictions is to operate successfully. The *individual unconscious* with which Freud deals refers to those contents which an individual represses for reasons of individual circumstances peculiar to his personal life situation. Freud deals to some extent with the social unconscious when he talks about the repression of incestuous strivings as being characteristic of all civilization; but in his clinical work, he mainly deals with the individual unconscious, and little attention is paid by most analysts to the social unconscious. [. . .]

For any experience to come into awareness, it must be comprehensible in accordance with the categories in which conscious thought is organized. I can become aware of any occurrence, inside or outside of myself, only when it can be linked with the system of categories in which I perceive. Some of the categories, such as time and space, may be universal, and may constitute categories of perception common to all men. Others, such as causality, may be a valid category for many, but not for all forms of conscious perception. Other categories are even less general and differ from culture to culture. For instance, in a preindustrial culture people may not perceive certain things in terms of their commercial value, while they do so in an industrial system. However this may be, experience can enter into awareness only under the condition that it can be perceived, related, and ordered in terms of a conceptual system and of its categories. This system is in itself a result of social evolution. Every society, by its own practice of living and by the mode of relatedness, of feeling and perceiving, develops a system, or categories, which determines the forms of awareness. This system works, as it were, like a *socially conditioned filter*: Experience cannot enter awareness unless it can penetrate this filter.

The question, then, is to understand more concretely how this "social filter" operates, and how it happens that it permits certain experiences to be filtered through while others are stopped from entering awareness.

First of all, we must consider that many experiences do not lend themselves easily to being perceived in awareness. Pain is perhaps the physical experience which best lends itself to being consciously perceived; sexual desire, hunger, etc., also are easily perceived; quite obviously, all sensations which are relevant to individual or group survival have easy access to awareness. But when it comes to a more subtle or complex experience, like *"seeing a rosebud in the early morning, a drop of dew on it, while the air is still chilly, the sun coming up, a bird singing"*—this is an experience which, in some cultures, easily lends itself to awareness (for instance, in Japan), while in modern Western culture this same experience will usually not come into awareness because it is not sufficiently "important" or "eventful" to be noticed. Whether or not subtle affective experiences can arrive at awareness depends on the degree to which such experiences are cultivated in a given culture. There are many affective experiences for which a given language has no word, while another language may be rich in words which express these feelings. In a language in which different affective experiences are not expressed by different words, it is almost impossible for one's experiences to come to clear awareness. Generally speaking, it may be said that an experience rarely comes into awareness for which the language has no word.

This fact is of special relevance with regard to such experiences which do not fit into our intellectual rational scheme of things. In English, for instance, the word *awe* (like in Hebrew *nora*) means two different things. Awe is the feeling of intense fright as it is still indicated in *awful*; and awe also means something like intense admiration, as we still find it in *awesome* (and in *awed by*). From a standpoint of conscious rational thought, fright and admiration are distinct feelings, hence they cannot be denoted by the same word; and if there is one word like awe, it is used in the one *or* the other sense, and the fact is forgotten that it actually means fright *and* admiration. In our *feeling* experience, however, fright and admiration are by no means mutually exclusive. On the contrary, as a visceral experience, fear and admiration are frequently part of one complex feeling, which, however, modern man is usually not aware of as such. It seems that the language of peoples who emphasized less than we do the intellectual aspect of experience had more words which expressed the feeling as such, while our modern languages tend to express only such feelings which can stand the test of our kind of logic. Incidentally, this phenomenon constitutes one of the greatest difficulties for dynamic psychology. Our language just does not give us the words which we need to describe many visceral experiences which do not fit our scheme of thoughts. Hence psychoanalysis has really no adequate language at its disposal. It could do what some other sciences have done and use symbols to denote certain complex feelings. For instance,

$$\frac{a}{t}$$

could stand for that complex feeling of admiration and terror which as once expressed by one word. Or

$$xy$$

could stand for the feeling of "aggressive defiance, superiority, accusation + hurt innocence, martyrdom, being persecuted and falsely accused." Again, this latter feeling is not a synthesis of different feelings, as our language would make us believe, but one specific feeling which can be observed in oneself and in others once one transcends the barrier of the assumption that nothing can be felt which cannot be "thought." If one does not use abstract symbols, the most adequate, paradoxically enough, scientific language for psychoanalysis is actually that of symbolism, poetry, or reference to themes of mythology. (Freud often chose the. latter way.) But if the psychoanalyst thinks he can be scientific by using technical terms of our language to denote emotional phenomena, he deceives himself and speaks of abstract constructs which do not correspond to the reality of felt experience.

But this is only one aspect of the filtering function of language. Different languages differ not only by the fact that they vary in the diversity of words they use to denote certain affective experiences, but also by their syntax, their grammar, and the root-meaning of their words. The whole language contains an attitude of life, is a frozen expression of experiencing life in a certain way.[1]

1. Cf. Benjamin Whorf, *Collected Papers on Metalinguistics* (Washington, D.C.: Foreign Service Institute, 1952).

Here are a few examples. There are languages in which the verb form "it rains," for instance, is conjugated differently depending on whether I say that it rains because I have been out in the rain and have got wet, or because I have seen it raining from the inside of a hut, or because somebody has told me that it rains. It is quite obvious that the emphasis of the language on these different *sources* of experiencing a fact (in this case, that it rains) has a deep influence on *the way* people experience facts. (In our modern culture, for instance, with its emphasis on the purely intellectual side of knowledge, it makes little difference how I know a fact, whether from direct or indirect experience, or from hearsay.) Or, in Hebrew, the main principle of conjugation is to determine whether an activity is complete (perfect) or incomplete (imperfect), while the time in which it occurs—past, present, future—is expressed only in a secondary fashion. In Latin both principles (time and perfection) are used together, while in English we are predominantly oriented in the sense of time. Again it goes without saying that this difference in conjugation expresses a difference in experiencing. (The significance of this difference becomes quite apparent in the English and German translations of the Old Testament. Often when the Hebrew text uses the perfect tense for an emotional experience like loving, meaning, "I love fully," the translator misunderstands and writes, "I loved.")

Still another example is to be found in the different uses of verbs and nouns in various languages, or even among different people speaking the same language. The noun refers to a "thing"; the verb refers to an activity. An increasing number of people prefer to think in terms of *having things*, instead of *being* or *acting*; hence, they prefer nouns to verbs.

Language, by its words, its grammar, its syntax, by the whole spirit which is frozen in it, determines which experiences penetrate to our awareness.

The second aspect of the filter which makes awareness possible is the *logic* which directs the thinking of people in a given culture. Just as most people assume that their language is "natural" and that other languages only use different words for the same things, they assume also that the rules which determine proper thinking are natural and universal ones; that what is illogical in one cultural system is illogical in any other because it conflicts with "natural" logic. A good example of this is the difference between Aristotelian and paradoxical logic.

Aristotelian logic is based on the law of identity (which states that A is A), the law of contradiction (A is not non-A), and the law of the excluded middle (A cannot be A *and* non-A, neither A *nor* non-A). Aristotle stated it: "It is impossible for the same thing at the same time to belong and not to belong to the same thing in the same respect.... This, then, is the most certain of all principles."[2]

In opposition to Aristotelian logic is what one might call *paradoxical logic*, which assumes that A and non-A do not exclude each other as predicates of X. Paradoxical logic was predominant in Chinese and Indian thinking, in Heraclitus' philosophy, and then again under the name of dialectics in the thought of Hegel and Marx. The general principle of paradoxical logic has been clearly described in general terms by Lao-tse: "Words that are strictly true seem to be paradoxical." And by Chuang-tzu: "That which is one is one. That which is not-one, is also one."[3]

Inasmuch as a person lives in a culture in which the correctness of Aristotelian logic is not doubted, it is exceedingly difficult, if not impossible, for him to be aware of experiences which contradict Aristotelian logic, hence which, from the standpoint of his culture, are nonsensical. A good example is Freud's concept of ambivalence, which says that one can experience love and hate for the same person at the same time. This experience, which from the standpoint of paradoxical logic is quite "logical," does not make sense from the standpoint of Aristotelian logic. As a result it is exceedingly difficult for most people to be aware of feelings of ambivalence. If they are aware of love, they cannot be aware of hate—since it would be utterly nonsensical to have two contradictory feelings at the same time toward the same person.

While language and logic are parts of the social filter which makes it difficult or impossible for an experience to enter awareness, the third part of the social filter is the most important one, for it is the one that does not *permit* certain feelings to reach consciousness and tends to expel them from this realm if they have reached it. It is made up by the social taboos, which declare certain ideas and feelings to be improper, forbidden, dangerous, and which prevent them from even reaching the level of consciousness.

An example taken from a primitive tribe may serve as an introduction to the problem indicated here. In a tribe of warriors, for instance, whose members live by killing and robbing the members of other tribes, there might be an individual who feels a revulsion against killing and robbing. Yet it is most unlikely that he will be aware of this feeling since it would be incompatible with that of the whole tribe; to be aware of this incompatible feeling would mean the danger of being completely isolated and

2. Aristotle, *Metaphysics*, Book Gamma, 1005b 20. Quoted from Aristotle's *Metaphysics*, trans. R. Hope (New York: Columbia University Press, 1952).
3. Cf. Lao-tse, *The Tâo Teh King: The Sacred Books of the East*, vol. 39, ed. Max Müller (London: Oxford University Press, 1927), 120.

ostracized. Hence an individual with such an experience of revulsion would probably develop a psychosomatic symptom such as vomiting, instead of letting the feeling of revulsion penetrate to his awareness. Exactly the contrary would be found in the case of a member of a peaceful agricultural tribe who has the impulse to go out and kill and rob members of other groups. He also would probably not permit himself to become aware of his impulses, but instead would develop a symptom—maybe intense fright.

Still another example, one from our own civilization: There must be many shopkeepers in our big cities who have a customer who badly needs, let us say, a suit of clothes, but who does not have sufficient money to buy even the cheapest one. Among those shopkeepers (especially the well-to-do ones) there must be a few who would have the natural human impulse to give the suit to the customer for the price that he can pay. But how many will permit themselves to be aware of such an impulse? I assume very few. The majority will repress it, and we might find among them quite a few who will have a dream during the following night which might express the repressed impulse in one form or another.

Another example: The modern "organization man" might feel that his life makes little sense, that he is bored by what he is doing, that he has little freedom to do and think as he sees fit, that he is chasing after an illusion of happiness which never comes true. But if he were aware of such feelings, he would be greatly hindered in his proper social functioning. Hence such awareness would constitute a real danger to society as it is organized; and as a result, the feeling is repressed.

Or, there must be many people who sense that it is irrational to buy a new car every two years and who might even have a feeling of sadness when they have to part from a car they have been using, one that has "grown on them." Yet if many were aware of such feelings, there would be danger that they would act on them—and where would our economy be, which is based on relentless consumption? Then again, is it possible that most people should be so lacking in natural intelligence that they do not see with how much incompetence many of their leaders—whatever the method by which they came to the top—perform their functions? Yet where would social cohesion and unified action be if such facts became conscious to more than a tiny minority? Is reality in this respect any different from what happens in Andersen's fairy tale of the emperor without clothes? Although the emperor is naked, only a little boy perceives this fact, while the rest of the people are convinced that the emperor is wearing beautiful clothes.

The irrationalities of any given society result in the necessity for its members to repress the awareness of many of their own feelings and observations. [...]

Why do people repress the awareness of what they would otherwise be aware of? Undoubtedly the main reason is fear. But fear of what? Is it fear of castration, as Freud assumed? There does not seem to be sufficient evidence to believe this. Is it fear of being killed, imprisoned, or fear of starvation? That might sound like a satisfactory answer, provided repression occurred only in systems of terror and oppression. But since this is not so, we have to inquire further. Are there more subtle fears which a society such as our own, for instance, produces? Let us think of a young executive or engineer in a big corporation. If he has thoughts which are not "sound," he might be inclined to repress them lest he might not get the kind of promotion others get. This, in itself, would be no tragedy, were it not for the fact that he, his wife, and his friends will consider him a "failure" if he falls behind in the competitive race. Thus the fear of being a failure can become a sufficient cause for repression.

But there is still another and, as I believe, the most powerful motive for repression: the *fear of isolation and ostracism*.

For man, inasmuch as he is *man*—that is to say, inasmuch as he transcends nature and is aware of himself and of death—the sense of complete aloneness and separateness is close to insanity. Man as man is afraid of insanity, just as man as animal is afraid of death. Man has to be related, he has to find union with others, in order to be sane. This need to be one with others is his strongest passion, stronger than sex and often even stronger than his wish to live. It is this fear of isolation and ostracism, rather than the "castration fear," that makes people repress the awareness of that which is taboo since such awareness would mean being different, separate, and hence, to be ostracized. For this reason the individual must blind himself from seeing that which his group claims does not exist, or accept as truth that which the majority says is true, even if his own eyes could convince him that it is false. The herd is so vitally important for the individual that their views, beliefs, feelings, constitute reality for him, more so than what his senses and his reason tell him. Just as in the hypnotic state of dissociation the hypnotist's voice and words take the place of reality, so the social pattern constitutes reality for most people. What man considers true, real, sane, are the clichés accepted by his society, and much that does not fit in with these clichés is excluded from awareness, is unconscious. There is almost nothing a man will not believe—or repress—when he is threatened with the explicit or implicit threat of ostracism. Returning to the fear of losing one's identity, which I discussed earlier, I want to state that for the majority of people, their identity is precisely rooted in their conformity with the social clichés. "They" are who they are supposed to be—hence the fear of ostracism implies the fear of the loss of identity, and the very combination of both fears has a most powerful effect.

The concept of ostracism as the basis of repression could lead to the rather hopeless view that every society can dehumanize and deform man in whatever way it likes because every society can always threaten him with ostracism. But to assume this would mean to forget another fact. Man is not only a member of society, but he is also a member of the human race. While man is afraid of complete isolation from his social group, he is also afraid of being isolated from the humanity which is inside him and which is represented by his conscience and his reason. To be completely inhuman is frightening, even when a whole society has adopted inhuman norms of behavior. The more human a society is, the less need is there for the individual to choose between isolation from society or from humanity. The greater the conflict between the social aims and human aims, the more is the individual torn between the two dangerous poles of isolation. To that degree to which a person—because of his own intellectual and spiritual development—feels his solidarity with humanity, can he tolerate social ostracism, and vice versa. The ability to act according to one's conscience depends on the degree to which one has transcended the limits of one's society and has become a citizen of the world.

The average individual does not permit himself to be aware of thoughts or feelings which are incompatible with the patterns of his culture, and hence he is forced to repress them. *Formally* speaking, then, what is unconscious and what is conscious depends on the structure of society and on the patterns of feeling and thought it produces. As to the *contents of the unconscious*, no generalization is possible. But one statement can be made: It always represents the whole man, with all his potentialities for darkness and light; it always contains the basis for the different answers which man is capable of giving to the question which existence poses. In the extreme case of the most regressive cultures, bent on returning to animal existence, this very wish is predominant and conscious, while all strivings to emerge from this level are repressed. In a culture which has moved from the regressive to the spiritual-progressive goal, the forces representing the dark are unconscious. But man, in any culture, has all the potentialities within himself; he is the archaic man, the beast of prey, the cannibal, the idolater, and he is the being with a capacity for reason, for love, for justice. The content of the unconscious, then, is neither the good nor the evil, the rational nor the irrational; it is both; it is all that is human. *The unconscious is the whole man—minus that part of him which corresponds to his society.* Consciousness represents social man, the accidental limitations set by the historical situation into which an individual is thrown. Unconsciousness represents universal man, the whole man, rooted in the cosmos; it represents the plant in him, the animal in him, the spirit in him; it represents his past, down to the dawn of human existence, and it represents his future up to the day when man will have become fully human, and when nature will be humanized as man will be "naturalized." To become aware of one's unconscious means to get in touch with one's full humanity and to do away with barriers which society erects within each man and, consequently, between each man and his fellow man. To attain this aim fully is difficult and a rare occurrence; to approximate it is in the grasp of everybody, as it constitutes the emancipation of man from the socially conditioned alienation from himself and humankind. Nationalism and xenophobia are the opposite poles to the humanistic experience brought about by becoming aware of one's unconscious.

11

The Sick Society:
On the Pathology of Normalcy

To speak of a whole society as lacking in mental health implies a controversial assumption contrary to the position of *sociological relativism* held by most social scientists today. They postulate that each society is normal inasmuch as it functions, and that pathology can be defined only in terms of the individual's lack of adjustment to the ways of life in his society.

To speak of a "sane society" implies a premise different from sociological relativism. It makes sense only if we assume that there can be a society which is *not* sane, and this assumption, in turn, implies that there are universal criteria for mental health which are valid for the human race as such, and according to which the state of health of each society can be judged. This position of *normative humanism* is based on a few fundamental premises.

The species "man" can be defined not only in anatomical and physiological terms; its members share basic *psychic* qualities, the laws which govern their mental and emotional functioning, and the aims for a satisfactory solution of the problem of human existence. It is true that our knowledge of man is still so incomplete that we cannot yet give a satisfactory definition of man in a psychological sense. It is the task of the "science of man" to arrive eventually at a correct description of what deserves to be called human nature. What has often been called "human nature" is but one of its many manifestations—and often a pathological one—and the function of such mistaken definition usually has been to defend a particular type of society as being the necessary outcome of man's mental constitution.

Against such reactionary use of the concept of human nature, the Liberals, since the eighteenth century, have stressed the malleability of human nature and the decisive influence of environmental factors. True and important as such emphasis is, it has led many social scientists to an assumption that man's mental constitution is a blank piece of paper, on which society and culture write their text, and which has no intrinsic quality of its own. This assumption is just as untenable and just as destructive of social progress as the opposite view was. The real problem is to infer the *core* common to the whole human race from the innumerable *manifestations* of human nature, the normal as well as the pathological ones, as we can observe them in different individuals and cultures. The task is furthermore to recognize the laws inherent in human nature and the inherent goals for its development and unfolding.

This concept of human nature is different from the way the term *human nature* is used conventionally. Just as man transforms the world around him, so he transforms himself in the process of history. He is his own creation, as it were. But just as he can only transform and modify the natural materials around him according to their nature, so he can only transform and modify himself according to his own nature. What man *does* in the process of history is to develop this potential, and to transform it according to its own possibilities. The point of view taken here is neither a "biological" nor a "sociological" one if that would mean separating these two aspects from each other. It is rather one transcending such dichotomy by the assumption that the main passions and drives in man result from the *total existence* of man, that they are definite and ascertainable, some of them conducive to health and happiness, others to sickness and unhappiness. Any given social order does not *create* these fundamental strivings but it determines which of the limited number of potential passions are to become manifest or dominant. Man as he appears in any given culture is always a manifestation of human nature, a manifestation, however, which in its specific outcome is determined by the social arrangements under which he lives. Just as the infant is born with all human potentialities, which are to develop under favorable social and cultural conditions, so the human race, in the process of history, develops into what it potentially is.

The approach of *normative humanism* is based on the assumption that, as in any other problem, there are right and wrong, satisfactory and unsatisfactory solutions to the problem of human existence. Mental health is achieved if man develops into full maturity according to the characteristics and laws of human nature. Mental illness consists in the failure of such development. From this premise the criterion of mental health is not one of individual adjustment to a given social order, but a universal one, valid for all men, of giving a satisfactory answer to the problem of human existence.

What is so deceptive about the state of mind of the members of a society is the "consensual validation" of their concepts. It is naively assumed that the fact that the majority of people share certain ideas or feelings proves the validity of these ideas and feelings. Nothing is further from the truth. Consensual validation as such has no bearing whatsoever on reason or mental health. Just as there is a *folie à deux* there is a *folie à millions*. The fact that millions of people share the same vices does not make these vices virtues, the fact that they share so many errors does not make the errors to be truths, and the fact that millions of people share the same forms of mental pathology does not make these people sane.

There is, however, an important difference between individual and social mental illness, which suggests a differentiation between two concepts: that of *defect*, and that of *neurosis*. If a person fails to attain freedom, spontaneity, a genuine expression of self, he may be considered to have a severe defect, provided we assume that freedom and spontaneity are the objective goals to be attained by every human being. If such a goal is not attained by the majority of members of any given society, we deal with the phenomenon of *socially patterned* defect. The individual shares it with many others; he is not aware of it as a defect, and his security is not threatened by the experience of being different, of being an outcast, as it were. What he may have lost in richness and in a genuine feeling of happiness, is made up by the security of fitting in with the rest of mankind—*as he knows them*. As a matter of fact, his very defect may have been raised to a virtue by his culture, and thus may give him an enhanced feeling of achievement.

An illustration is the feeling of guilt and anxiety which Calvin's doctrines aroused in men. It may be said that the person who is overwhelmed by a feeling of his own powerlessness and unworthiness, by unceasing doubt as to whether he is saved or condemned to eternal punishment, who is hardly capable of genuine joy, suffers from a severe defect. Yet this very defect was culturally patterned; it was looked upon as particularly valuable, and the individual was thus protected from the neurosis which he would have acquired in a culture where the same defect gave him a feeling of profound inadequacy and isolation.

Spinoza formulated the problem of the socially patterned defect very clearly. He says:

> Many people are seized by one and the same affect with great consistency. All his senses are so strongly affected by one object that he believes this object to be present even if it is not. If this happens while the person is awake, the person is believed to be insane. . . . But if the *greedy* person thinks only of money and possessions, the *ambitious* one

only of fame, one does not think of them as being insane, but only as annoying; generally one has contempt for them. But *factually* greediness, ambition, and so forth are forms of insanity, although usually one does not think of them as "illness."[1]

These words were written a few hundred years ago; they still hold true, although the defects have been culturally patterned to *such* an extent now that they are not even generally thought any more to be annoying or contemptible. Today we come across a person who acts and feels like an automaton; who never experiences anything which is really his; who experiences himself entirely as the person he thinks he is supposed to be; whose artificial smile has replaced genuine laughter; whose meaningless chatter has replaced communicative speech; whose dulled despair has taken the place of genuine pain. Two statements can be made about this person. One is that he suffers from a defect of spontaneity and individuality which may seem incurable. At the same time, it may be said that he does not differ essentially from millions of others who are in the same position. For most of them, the culture provides patterns which enable them *to live with a defect without becoming ill*. It is as if each culture provided the remedy against the outbreak of manifest neurotic symptoms which would result from the defect produced by it.

Suppose that in our Western culture movies, radios, television, sports events, and newspapers ceased to function for only four weeks. With these main avenues of escape closed, what would be the consequences for people thrown back upon their own resources? I have no doubt that even in this short time thousands of nervous breakdowns would occur, and many more thousands of people would be thrown into a state of acute anxiety, not different from the picture which is diagnosed clinically as "neurosis." If the opiate against the socially patterned defect were withdrawn, the manifest illness would make its appearance.

For a minority, the pattern provided by the culture does not work. They are often those whose individual defect is more severe than that of the average person, so that the culturally offered remedies are not sufficient to prevent the outbreak of manifest illness. (A case in point is the person whose aim in life is to attain power and fame. While this aim is, in itself, a pathological one, there is nevertheless a difference between the person who uses his powers to attain this aim realistically, and the more severely sick one who has so little emerged from his infantile grandiosity that he does not do anything toward the attainment of his goal but waits for a miracle to happen and, thus feeling more and more powerless, ends

1. Spinoza, *Ethics*, IV Prop. 44 Schol.

up in a feeling of futility and bitterness.) But there are also those whose character structure, and hence whose conflicts, differ from those of the majority, so that the remedies which are effective for most of their fellow men are of no help to them. Among this group we sometimes find people of greater integrity and sensitivity than the majority, who for this very reason are incapable of accepting the cultural opiate, while at the same time they are not strong and healthy enough to live soundly "against the stream."

The foregoing discussion on the difference between neurosis and the socially patterned defect may give the impression that if society only provides the remedies against the outbreak of manifest symptoms, all goes well, and it can continue to function smoothly, however great the defects created by it. History shows us, however, that this is not the case.

It is true, indeed, that man, in contrast to the animal, shows an almost infinite malleability; just as he can eat almost anything, live under practically any kind of climate and adjust himself to it, there is hardly any psychic condition which he cannot endure, and under which he cannot carry on. He can live free, and as a slave. Rich and in luxury, and under conditions of half-starvation. He can live as a warrior, and peaceably; as an exploiter and robber, and as a member of a cooperating and loving fellowship. There is hardly a psychic state in which man cannot live, and hardly anything which cannot be done with him, and for which he cannot be used. All these considerations seem to justify the assumption that there is no such thing as a nature common to all men, and that would mean in fact that there is no such thing as a species "man," except in a physiological and anatomical sense.

Yet, in spite of all this evidence, the history of man shows that we have omitted one fact. Despots and ruling cliques can succeed in dominating and exploiting their fellow man, but they cannot prevent *reactions* to this inhuman treatment. Their subjects become frightened, suspicious, lonely and, if not due to external reasons, their systems collapse at some point because fears, suspicions, and loneliness eventually incapacitate the majority to function effectively and intelligently. Whole nations, or social groups within them, can be subjugated and exploited for a long time, but *they react*. They react with apathy or such impairment of intelligence, initiative, and skills that they gradually fail to perform the functions which should serve their rulers. Or they react by the accumulation of such hate and destructiveness as to bring about an end to themselves, their rulers, and their system. Again their reaction may create such independence and longing for freedom that a better society is built upon their creative impulses. Which reaction occurs depends on many factors: on economic and political ones, and on the spiritual climate in which people live. But whatever the reactions are, the statement that man can live under almost any condition is only half true; it must be supplemented by the other statement, that if he lives under conditions which are contrary to his nature and to the basic requirements for human growth and sanity, he cannot help reacting; he must either deteriorate and perish, or bring about conditions which are more in accordance with his needs.

12

Steps to a New Society

In the various critical analyses of capitalism we find remarkable agreement. While it is true that the capitalism of the nineteenth century was criticized for its neglect of the material welfare of the workers, this was never the main criticism. What Owen and Proudhon, Tolstoy and Bakunin, Durkheim and Marx, Einstein and Schweitzer talk about is *man*, and what happens to him in our industrial system. Although they express it in different concepts, they all find that man has lost his central place, that he has been made an instrument for the purposes of economic aims, that he has been estranged from, and has lost the concrete relatedness to, his fellow men and to nature, that he has ceased to have a meaningful life. I have tried to express the same idea by elaborating on the concept of alienation and by showing psychologically what the psychological results of alienation are; that man regresses to a receptive and marketing orientation and ceases to be productive; that he loses his sense of self, becomes dependent on approval, hence tends to conform and yet to feel insecure; he is dissatisfied, bored, and anxious, and spends most of his energy in the attempt to compensate for or just to cover up this anxiety. His intelligence is excellent, his reason deteriorates, and in view of his technical powers he is seriously endangering the existence of civilization, and even of the human race.

If we turn to views about the *causes* for this development, we find less agreement than in the diagnosis of the illness itself. While the early nineteenth century was still prone to see the causes of all evil in the lack of *political* freedom, and especially of universal suffrage, the socialists, and especially the Marxists stressed the significance of economic factors. They believed that the alienation of man resulted from his role as an object of exploitation and use. Thinkers like Tolstoy and Burckhardt, on the other hand, stressed the spiritual and moral impoverishment as the cause of Western man's decay; Freud believed that modern man's trouble was the overrepression of his instinctual drives and the resulting neurotic manifestations. But any explanation which analyzes one sector to the exclusion of others is unbalanced, and thus wrong. The socioeconomic, spiritual, and psychological explanations look at the same phenomenon from different aspects, and the very task of a theoretical analysis is to see how these different aspects are interrelated, and how they interact.

What holds true for the causes holds, of course, true for the remedies by which modern man's defect can be cured. If I believe that "the" cause of the illness is economic, *or* spiritual, *or* psychological, I necessarily believe that remedying "the" cause leads to sanity. On the other hand, if I see how the various aspects are interrelated, I shall arrive at the conclusion that sanity and mental health can be attained only by simultaneous changes in the sphere of industrial and political organization, of spiritual and philosophical orientation, of character structure, and of cultural activities. The concentration of effort in any of these spheres, to the exclusion or neglect of others, is destructive of *all* change. In fact, here seems to lie one of the most important obstacles to the progress of mankind. Christianity has preached spiritual renewal, neglecting the changes in the social order without which spiritual renewal must remain ineffective for the majority of people. The age of enlightenment has postulated as the highest norms independent judgment and reason; it preached political equality without seeing that political equality could not lead to the realization of the brotherhood of man if it was not accompanied by a fundamental change in the social-economic organization. Socialism, and especially Marxism, has stressed the necessity for social and economic changes, and neglected the necessity of the inner change in human beings, without which economic change can never lead to the "good society." Each of these great reform movements of the last two thousand years has emphasized one sector of life to the exclusion of the others; their proposals for reform and renewal were radical—but their results were almost complete failure. The preaching of the gospel led to the establishment of the Catholic church; the teachings of the rationalists of the eighteenth century to Robespierre and Napoleon; the doctrines of Marx to Stalin. The results could hardly have been different. Man is a unit; his thinking, feeling, and his practice of life are inseparably connected. He cannot be free in his thought when he is not free emotionally; and he cannot be free emotionally if he is dependent and unfree in his practice of life, in his economic and social relations. Trying to advance radically in one sector to the exclusion of others must necessarily lead to the result to which it did lead, namely, that the radical demands in one sphere are fulfilled only by a few individuals, while for the majority they become formulae and rituals, serving to cover up the fact that in other spheres nothing has changed. Undoubtedly *one* step of integrated progress in all spheres of life will have more far-reaching and more lasting results for the progress of the human race than a hundred steps preached—and even for a short while lived—in only one isolated sphere. Several thousands of years of failure in "isolated progress" should be a rather convincing lesson.

Closely related to this problem is that of *radicalism* and *reform*, which seems to form such a dividing line between various political solutions. Yet, a closer analysis can show that this differentiation as it is usually conceived of is deceptive. There is reform and reform; reform can be *radical*, that is, going to the roots, or it can be superficial, trying to patch up symptoms without touching the causes. Reform which is not radical, in this sense, never accomplishes its ends and eventually ends up in the opposite direction. So-called radicalism, on the other hand, which believes that we can solve problems by force, when observation, patience, and continuous activity are required, is as unrealistic and fictitious as reform. Historically speaking, they both often lead to the same result. The revolution of the Bolsheviks led to Stalinism, the reform of the right-wing Social Democrats in Germany led to Hitler. The true criterion of reform is not its tempo but its realism, its true "radicalism"; it is the question whether it goes to the roots and attempts to change causes—or whether it remains on the surface and attempts to deal only with symptoms.

If this chapter is to discuss roads to sanity, that is, methods of cure, we had better pause here for a moment and ask ourselves what we know about the nature of cure in cases of individual mental diseases. The cure of social pathology must follow the same principle, since it is the pathology of so many human beings, and not of an entity beyond or apart from individuals.

The conditions for the cure of individual pathology are mainly the following:

1. A development must have occurred which is contrary to the proper functioning of the psyche. In Freud's theory this means that the libido has failed to develop normally and that as a result, symptoms are produced. In the frame of reference of humanistic psychoanalysis, the causes of pathology lie in the failure to develop a productive orientation, a failure which results in the development of irrational passions, especially of incestuous, destructive, and exploitative strivings. The *fact* of suffering,

whether it is conscious or unconscious, resulting from the failure of normal development, produces a dynamic *striving to overcome the suffering*, that is, *for change in the direction of health*. This striving for health in our physical as well as in our mental organism is the basis for any cure of sickness, and it is absent only in the most severe pathology.

2. The first step necessary to permit this tendency for health to operate is the *awareness* of the suffering and of that which is shut out and disassociated from our conscious personality. In Freud's doctrine, repression refers mainly to *sexual* strivings. In our frame of reference, it refers to the repressed irrational passions, to the repressed feeling of aloneness and futility, and to the longing for love and productivity, which is also repressed.

3. Increasing self-awareness can become fully effective only if a next step is taken, that of changing a practice of life which was built on the basis of the neurotic structure, and which reproduces it constantly. A patient, for instance, whose neurotic character makes him want to submit to parental authorities has usually constructed a life where he has chosen dominating or sadistic father images as bosses, teachers, and so on. He will be cured only if he changes his realistic life situation in such a way that it does not constantly reproduce the submissive tendencies he wants to give up. Furthermore, he must change his systems of values, norms, and ideals, so that they further rather than block his striving for health and maturity.

The same conditions—*conflict* with the requirements of human nature and resulting suffering, *awareness* of what is shut out, and *change* of the realistic situation and of values and norms—are also necessary for a cure of *social* pathology. [...]

❖   ❖   ❖

The conclusion seems unavoidable that the ideas of activation, responsibility, participation—that is, of the humanization of technological society—can find full expression only in a *movement* which is not bureaucratic, not connected with the political machines, and which is the result of active and imaginative efforts by those who share the same aims. Such a movement itself, in its organization and method, would be expressive of the aim to which it is devoted: to educate its members for the new kind of society in the process of striving for it.

In the following, I will try to describe three different forms of this movement.

The first step would be the formation of a National Council, which could be called the "Voice of American Conscience." I think of a group of, say, fifty Americans whose integrity and capability are unquestioned. While they might have different religious and political convictions, they would share the humanist aims which are the basis for the humanization of technological society. They would deliberate and issue statements which, because of the weight of those who issued them, would be newsworthy, and because of the truth and rationality of their contents would win attention from at least a large sector of the American public. Such councils could also be formed on a local level, dealing with the general questions but specifically with the practical questions relevant for the city or state which they represented. One could imagine that there might be a whole organization of Councils of the Voice of American Conscience, with a nationally representative group and many local groups following basically the same aims.

The National Council would deal with the broad aspects of national affairs, that is, foreign and domestic policies, while the local councils would take up the questions relevant to state and communities, again concerned with broad aspects rather than with details of execution. For example, the National Council would debate the question of the Vietnam War, our foreign policy in Asia, our assistance to the development of the poor nations, the reconstruction of our cities, the problems of values, education, and culture. The local councils would debate problems of conservation, city planning, slum clearance, relocating industries, etc. These debates would not be conducted on a general and abstract level. On the contrary, they would constitute the best thinking of the best minds in America. Often the council would form subcommittees to study special problems and call upon specialists for advice. It would be up to the Voice of American Conscience (1) to clarify the issues, (2) to show the real possibilities and alternatives, (3) to recommend solutions, (4) to respond to statements and actions by other important social bodies, and to any criticism of their own recommendations. The examination of the issues and the recommended solutions would be rooted in the rationality and humanist values which the best in American culture stands for. These councils would balance the structure based on political power represented by the government, the legislature, and the political parties. They would be the voice of reason and conscience, addressing themselves to the organs of power and to the population as a whole. Whenever the councils did not arrive at unanimous solutions, one or more minority reports would be issued.

It is easy to underestimate what such councils could do by pointing out that they would have no power. This is true in an obvious sense; it is not quite so true in a more subtle sense. Technological society, more than any society before, rests upon knowledge, on education in science and rational thought. While the average professional is not a true scientist but a mere technician, the development of scientific ideas depends on the development of the whole system of rational thought and reason. Development of technique has its basis in the development of scientific theory; this means that economic and political progress rests in the long run on the progress of culture. Those who represent culture have no direct power; but since the progress of society depends on their contribution, their voice will be taken seriously by a new class of people with college educations (teachers, technicians, programmers, laboratorians, research workers, professionals, etc.) whose cooperation is a vital necessity for the functioning of the social system.

As to the composition of the councils, they should not only represent various shades of political, religious, and philosophical convictions but also various fields of activities. Natural and social scientists, individuals from the fields of government, business, management sciences, philosophers, theologians, and artists should be among the members. But the foremost principle is the integrity and accomplishment of the members, which override the principle of a well-balanced composition. It hardly needs to be added that the members of these councils must be persons with a deep concern for the public weal, and hence willing to spend time and energy on their work in the councils.

It is not too farfetched to think that the moral and intellectual weight of such groups could be of considerable influence on the thinking of Americans and by the freshness of its approach attract a great deal of attention.

How would the members of the council be chosen? Quite obviously, they would not be elected as candidates are elected in a political party. And they couldn't very well be appointed by one supreme figure either, since that would give undue power to one individual. However, the formation of the National Council and of the local councils appears to be so difficult only if one is caught in the old alternative between free election or arbitrary appointment. If one liberates oneself from these alternatives and thinks imaginatively, one will discover that there are methods which are perfectly feasible—although not as neat as the traditional ones. There are quite a number of people known for their integrity and achievement, and it would not be particularly difficult for a group of, let us say, ten to agree on the names of forty or fifty people who should be invited, by asking others who combine wisdom and intelligence what their preferences would be. Naturally, the forty or fifty people who were approached would themselves indicate who among those suggested were unacceptable to them. As a result of this procedure, one might get a National Council which would not satisfy everybody and yet which would be fundamentally representative of the American conscience. The method of forming this council is nonbureaucratic, personalistic, concrete, and, for this very reason, more effective than the traditional methods. The regional and local councils could be formed in the same way, possibly aided by suggestions from the members of the National Council.

The councils, of course, do not satisfy the needs which have been mentioned before: the need of the individual to work actively together with others, to talk, plan, and act together, to do something which is meaningful beyond the money-making activities of everyday life. To relate in a less alienated fashion than is customary in most relations to others, to make sacrifices, to put into practice norms and values in everyday life, to be open and "vulnerable," to be imaginative, to rely on one's own judgment and decision, the formation of a new type of social group is necessary.

I propose that this kind of shared activity and interest could occur on two levels: in larger groups of one hundred to three hundred members who would form "clubs," and in much smaller "groups" of about twenty-five members, which would follow the same principle but in a much more intensive and absorbing way.

The clubs should, if possible, be mixed in age and social class—but only experience would show to what extent practical considerations might make such a mixture difficult; it might be necessary that the clubs be relatively homogeneous, but this defect could be made up for by an arrangement whereby clubs with very different kinds of memberships could meet together regularly to exchange views and have personal contact. The clubs should have a permanent meeting place; this could be a storefront or a basement—which is possible even in the poorest sections—or a school, church, or other building which could be rented at a fee contributed by the members. The meetings, which might take place once a week, should be meetings for exchanging information, discussion, and planning for the dissemination of the ideas of the movement. There should also be some relevant practical work undertaken by all members, such as participation in political campaigns, organization of discussion groups among neighbors and friends, engaging political leaders in public debates, problem-oriented care of public functions and community property, care of people—the old, children, and people in trouble—in the spirit of concern and stimulation rather than of bureaucratic methods. (It has been amply demonstrated that there are many people without degrees who, by their talent and skill, do as good or better work with and for others than the specialists. I mention as only one example Mayor John Lindsay's program for the rehabilitation of addicts in New York City; in this program specially gifted people—not professional personnel—and former addicts have been very successful in the most important educative-therapeutic function.) The groups would have their own cultural life: showing movies, discussing books and ideas, dance, music, art—all of an active and nonconsumer type.

It is of the greatest importance that these clubs try to have a style of their own, different from the style of traditional political or cultural clubs. The discussions should be led in such a way that the issues are clarified rather than obscured by phraseology and ideology. There must be a sufficient number of people in each club who are aware of the pitfalls of language, are on the watch for obscuring or ideological language, and can teach how to think and to speak realistically. It is to be hoped that through this style of expressing oneself, the unnecessary misunderstandings and the accompanying defensive and attacking attitudes will be reduced considerably, and that people will learn to concentrate on their interest in what they are talking about rather than on their egos—which maintain opinions like flags that have to be defended. One would assume that out of this will develop personal contact more serious than that which is usual among conventional groups or even in what are often called personal friendships.

Needless to say, the organization of these clubs must be free from all bureaucratic procedure. Each should have a chairman and a secretary, and these offices should change among the members every year. It would seem to be useful if once every six months or every year the representatives of the clubs—say, one for each club—could meet regionally and nationally in order to exchange experiences and to demonstrate to the rest of the population the value and fruitfulness of this type of organization.

They might be united by a loose and informal organization which helped to establish contact between the clubs, responded to requests for advice and help, organized common meetings, and represented the clubs to the public. But each club should retain full autonomy, and be completely free from interference and control from above. Considering this autonomy, the various clubs would differ a great deal among themselves, and each individual could choose to join the club whose spirit and program was most congenial to him. As to the formation of these clubs, the only feasible way is that of spontaneous action. One or two persons who were seriously interested in the formation of a club could invite five or ten others and from this nucleus a large group of from one hundred to three hundred persons might grow.

The question must be raised why the clubs should not be a part of a political party, like Tammany Hall, for example, within the Democratic party. There are mainly two reasons why this would be a mistake. The first and more obvious one is that none of the existing parties represents a philosophy and attitude like those that would underlie and be carried on by the clubs. Both parties (and even a third party) would have members and sympathizers who shared the aims of the clubs while they differed in their party affiliation. To have the clubs politically unified would mean losing many people who either belong to another party or have no sympathy for political parties at all.

The second reason is based on the very nature of the movement and the clubs. Their function would be not simply to influence political action, but to create a new attitude, to transform people, to demonstrate new ideas as they appeared in the flesh, as it were, of many groups of people, and thus to influence other people more effectively than is possible by political concepts. The new movement would be a cultural movement, aiming at the transformation of persons and of our whole culture; it would be concerned with socioeconomic and political matters, but also with interpersonal relations, art, language, style of life, and values. The clubs are meant to be cultural, social, and personalistic centers, and hence to go far beyond what a political club could aspire to do; they would also arouse a greater or at least a different kind of allegiance than political clubs do.

While the clubs would be basically different from political organizations, they would not be indifferent to politics. On the contrary, they would engage in clarifying and seriously discussing political issues; they would attempt to point to the real issues and to unmask deceptive rhetoric; their members would try to influence those political groups they might belong to and encourage a new spirit in politics.

There is also the possibility that a number of clubs would spring from groups which already exist, like certain religious, political, or professional groups, and either that the first clubs would consist mainly of the members of such groups, or that these members would form the nucleus of groups which would try to attract people outside of their own organizations.

I believe that these clubs could form the basis for a mass movement of people. They would form a home for those who are genuinely interested in the aims of the movement and who want to further it, but who are not as totally and radically committed as a small number of people might be.

For this more radically committed minority, another form of common life and action seems desirable and necessary, which for the lack of a better word may be called "groups."

Any attempt to spell out new forms of living or group activities such as the ones which are envisaged in the "groups" must necessarily fail. To some extent this holds true even for describing the clubs; but when we speak about the groups who would try to achieve a new style of life, a new consciousness, a new language in a more radical way than the clubs will do, the right words must be lacking to the same extent that the qualities of the life in the groups are new. It is easier, of course, to say what the groups would *not* be like. There has been a great deal of group activity emerging in recent years, from group therapy to "contact" groups to hippie groups of various kinds. The groups envisaged here are very different. Their members would share a new philosophy, a philosophy of the love of life, its manifestations in human relations, politics, art, social organization. What would be characteristic of them is that none of these areas of human activities is isolated from each other, but each aspect gets its meaning by being related to all others.

PART V

Another View of Human Nature

Fromm is often linked with existentialist philosophy, because he reflected on the origins of the human situation and drew conclusions about human nature. Although these descriptions are accurate, Fromm's interest was not primarily existentialist. His concern is with man's psychological state at the point of his differentiation from the animal kingdom. The need to make this state the starting point of all further reflection on human nature arose out of his criticism of Freud's theory of drives. In contrast to Freud, Fromm assumed that the drives that shape our relationships to other people and the world do not originate in sexual drives but have an independent existence as "psychic drives." By doing so, Fromm postulated the existence of a psychological dimension of human nature independent of both the physical and the intellectual dimensions and operating according to its own laws. Fromm's first major book, *Escape from Freedom* (1941), is based on this revised view of human nature, but it is not discussed in detail until *The Sane Society* (1955) and in several shorter articles on the psychoanalytic view of human nature and humanism.

Man is distinguished from animals by his psychological dimension, so reflection on the original psychological state of man as he evolved represents the only appropriate starting point for drawing conclusions about human nature. An approach via "psychological man" has a variety of consequences for our view of human nature as a whole. The following texts are intended to illustrate a few of them. They are concerned with a holistic view of man, the dialectical dynamics of all human development, the capacity to love and create culture, and the corresponding roles of self-love and love for one's fellow man. It is in his view of the latter that Fromm's view of human nature departs most noticeably from the prevailing modern view, which stresses man's "natural" hostile tendencies toward his own kind.

13

On the Search for the Nature of Man

For most of the thinkers of Greek antiquity, of the Middle Ages, and up to the period of Kant, it was self-evident that there is something called human nature, something that philosophically speaking constitutes the "essence of man." There were various views about what constitutes this essence, but there was agreement that such an essence exists—that is to say, that there is something by virtue of which man is man.

But during the last hundred years, or even longer, this traditional view began to be questioned. One reason for this change was the increasing emphasis given to the historical approach to man. An examination of the history of humanity suggests that man in our epoch is so different from man in previous ones that it is unrealistic to assume that men in every historical epoch have had in common that essence which can be called "human nature." The historical approach was reinforced in this century by studies in the field of cultural anthropology. The study of the so-called primitive peoples has shown such a diversity of customs, values, feelings, and thoughts that many anthropologists arrived at the concept that man is born as a blank sheet of paper on which each culture writes its text. To these influences of the historical and anthropological approaches was added that of the evolutionary one, which also tended to shake the belief in a common "human nature." Lamarck and, more precisely, Darwin and other biologists showed that all living beings are subject to evolutionary change. Modern physics has undertaken to demonstrate that the physical world also evolves and changes. Without any metaphor we can say that the totality of the world is a totality in movement, a totality that, as A. N. Whitehead would say, finds itself in a state of "process."

One other factor contributed to the tendency to deny the phenomenon of a fixed human nature, of an essence of man. The concept of human nature has been abused so often, has been used as a shield behind which the worst injustices are committed, that when we hear it mentioned we are inclined to seriously doubt its moral value, and even its sense. In the name of human nature Plato, Aristotle, and most of the thinkers up to the eighteenth century defended slavery (exceptions among the Greeks would be the Stoics, defenders of the equality of all men; in the Renaissance, such humanists as Erasmus, Thomas More, or Juan Luis Vives); in its name, nationalism and racism were born; in the name of a supposedly superior Aryan nature, the Nazis exterminated more than six million human beings; in the name of a certain abstract nature, the white man feels superior to the Negro, the powerful to the helpless, the strong to the weak. "Human nature," in our days, too often has been made to serve the purposes of state and society.

Is it necessary to come to the conclusion that there is no human nature? Such an assumption seems to imply as many dangers as those inherent in the concept of a fixed nature. If there were no essence common to all men, it may be argued there could be no unity of men, there could be no value or norms valid for all men, there could not even be the science of psychology or anthropology, which has as its subject matter "man." Are we not then caught between two undesirable and dangerous assumptions: the reactionary view of assuming a fixed and unalterable human nature, and the relativistic one that leads to the conclusion that man shares with other men only his anatomical and physiological attributes?

Perhaps it would be helpful to distinguish between the concept of the nature, or essence, of man and that of certain attributes of man common to all, and yet which in themselves may not constitute a full concept of the nature or essence of man. We can call these *essential attributes*, that is to say, attributes that belong to man qua man, and yet distinguish them from the "essence" of man, which may comprise all these essential attributes or more, and may possibly be defined as something from which the various attributes follow. [...]

These attributes of man—reason, the capacity for production, the creation of social organization, and the capacity for symbolmaking—are, indeed, essential although they do not constitute the totality of human nature. But they are general human potentialities and may not constitute what could be called "human nature." Given all of these attributes, man could be free or determined, good or evil, driven by greed or by ideals; there could be laws to govern his nature or there could be no such laws; all men could have a common nature, aside from these attributes, or they might not share in such a common nature; there may be values common to all men, or there may not be. In short, we are still faced with the problem we raised in the beginning: Is there, aside from certain general attributes, something that could be called human nature, or the essence of man?

One approach that is relatively recent seems to be helpful in the solution of our problem, but at the same time it seems to complicate it. A number of philosophers, from Kierkegaard and Marx to William James, Bergson, and Teilhard de Chardin, have perceived that man *makes himself*; that man is the author of his own history. In earlier ages life in this world has been conceived as extending from the creation to the end of the universe, and man is a being placed in the world in order to find either salvation or condemnation at any moment during his lifetime. Time, however, has come to play a central role in the philosophy and psychology of our days. Marx saw in history a constant process of man making himself as an individual and as a species; William James considered that the life of the spirit is the "stream of consciousness"; Bergson believed that in the very depth of our soul we are "duration," that is, personal and intransferable time that has been lived; the existentialists, on their part, have told us that we lack an essence, that we are in the first instance an existence, that is, that we are that which we make of ourselves during the course of our life.

Well now, if man is historical and temporal, if he constructs or makes himself as he changes and modifies in and within time, it would seem evident that we can no longer talk of a "human nature," of an "essence of man." Man no longer *is* rational; he *becomes* rational. He no longer *is* social; he *becomes* social. He no longer *is* religious; he *becomes* religious. And what about human nature? Can we still refer to it?

We propose to take a position that seems to us to be the most adequate and empirical answer to the problem of human nature, and that seems the most adequate to overcome the difficulties caused by the two extreme positions—that of the fixed or unalterable human nature, and that of a lack of anything that is common to all men, with the exception of some essential attributes. [. . .]

The essence, or nature, of man is seen in certain contradictions inherent in human—as against animal—existence. Man is an animal, but without having sufficient instincts to direct his actions. He not only has intelligence—as has the animal—but also self-awareness; yet he has not the power to escape the dictates of his nature. He is a "freak of nature," being in nature and at the same time transcending it. These contradictions create conflict and fright, a disequilibrium which man must try to solve in order to achieve a better equilibrium. But having reached this, new contradictions emerge and thus again necessitate the search for a new equilibrium, and so forth. In other words, the questions, not the answers, are man's "essence." The answers, trying to solve the dichotomies, lead to various manifestations of human nature. The dichotomies and the resulting disequilibrium are an ineradicable part of man qua man; the various kinds of solutions of these contradictions depend on socioeconomic, cultural, and psychic factors; however, they are by no means arbitrary and indefinite. There is a limited number of answers which have either been reached or anticipated in human history. These answers, while determined by historical circumstances, differ at the same time in terms of these solutions, differ in terms of their adequacy to enhance human vitality, strength, joy, and courage. The fact that the solutions depend on many factors does not exclude that human insight and will can work toward attempting to reach better rather than worse solutions.

Summing up, it can be stated that there is a significant consensus among those who have examined the nature of man. It is believed that man has to be looked upon in all his concreteness as a physical being placed in a specific psychical and social world with all the limitations and weaknesses that follow from this aspect of his existence. At the same time he is the only creature in whom life has become aware of itself, who has an ever-increasing awareness of himself and the world around him, and who has the possibilities for the development of new capacities, material and spiritual, which make his life an open road with a determinable end. As Pascal said, if man is the weakest of all beings, if he is nothing but a "reed," he is also the center of the universe, because he is a "thinking reed."

Of course man is not wholly definable, but what we have termed his "essential attributes" can give us an approximate, and at the same time, rather accurate approach, to what we may call his nature. Now, human nature is not only a principle, but it is also a capacity. In other words, man tends to achieve his being inasmuch as he develops love and reason. We could say that man is able to love and reason because he is but also, and conversely, that he is because he is capable of reasoning and loving. The capacity to become aware, to give account to himself of himself and of his existential situation, makes him human; this capacity is fundamentally his nature.

This is what many of the great philosophers, mystics, and theologians of the East and the West have believed. For all of them there is within man a *spiritual* reality that is born, precisely because he can know himself and others, and that is a part of life itself. It should not be believed, however, that only those philosophers known as *spiritualists* uphold this point of view. By means of other forms of conceptualization, many of the so-called materialists uphold, precisely, that this existential conflict is the basis of human life. Such is the case with Democritus in Greece; such is the case with the Greek skeptics, for whom what mattered was not to speak, but the silence of contemplation; such is the case with Feuerbach and Marx, for whom man is an end in itself.

Finally we must distinguish between those who think that man is an end in itself, and those who believe that man, like all other things in nature, is a means to other ends—the state, the family, wealth, power, etc. The reader will find that many of the great thinkers belong in the first group. For all these thinkers man is characterized by the capacity of being aware, of wondering, and of finding values and goals that are the optimal answer to the solution of his existential dichotomies. Whether these thinkers thought in theistic or nontheistic frames of reference, they all thought of man as a being whose greatness is rooted in his capacity to be aware of his limitations, and in this process of increasing awareness, to overcome them.

If we believe that man is not a thing and not a means for ends outside of himself, then, indeed, the understanding of man's nature has never been more difficult than in our contemporary industrial society. This society has achieved a mastery of nature through man's intellect that was undreamed of until only a century ago. Stimulated by his ever-increasing technical capacity, man has concentrated all his energies on the production and consumption of things. In this process he experiences himself as a thing, manipulating machines and being manipulated by them. If he is not exploited by others, he exploits himself; he uses his human essence as a means to serve his existence; his human powers as a means to satisfy his ever-expanding and, to a large extent, artificial material needs. There is a danger, then, that man may forget he is a man. Hence, the reconsideration of the tradition of thought about the nature of man was never more difficult, but at the same time never more necessary than it is today.

14

Freedom and the Growth of the Self

The social history of man started with his emerging from a state of one-ness with the natural world to an awareness of himself as an entity separate from surrounding nature and men. Yet this awareness remained very dim over long periods of history. The individual continued to be closely tied to the natural and social world from which he emerged; while being partly aware of himself as a separate entity, he felt also part of the world around him. The growing process of the emergence of the individual from his original ties, a process which we may call "individuation," seems to have reached its peak in modern history in the centuries between the Reformation and the present.

In the life history of an individual we find the same process. A child is born when it is no longer one with its mother and becomes a biological entity separate from her. Yet, while this biological separation is the beginning of individual human existence, the child remains functionally one with its mother for a considerable period.

To the degree to which the individual, figuratively speaking, has not yet completely severed the umbilical cord which fastens him to the outside world, he lacks freedom; but these ties give him security and a feeling of belonging and of being rooted somewhere. I wish to call these ties that exist before the process of individuation has resulted in the complete emergence of an individual "primary ties." They are organic in the sense that they are a part of normal human development; they imply a lack of individuality, but they also give security and orientation to the individual. They are the ties that connect the child with its mother, the member of a primitive community with his clan and nature, or the medieval man with the church and his social caste. Once the stage of complete individuation is reached and the individual is free from these primary ties, he is confronted with a new task: to orient and root himself in the world and to find security in other ways than those which were characteristic of his preindividualistic existence. Freedom then has a different meaning from the one it had before this stage of evolution is reached. It is necessary to stop here and to clarify these concepts by discussing them more concretely in connection with individual and social development.

The comparatively sudden change from fetal into human existence and the cutting off of the umbilical cord mark the independence of the infant from the mother's body. But this independence is only real in the crude sense of the separation of the two bodies. In a functional sense, the infant remains part of the mother. It is fed, carried, and taken care of in every vital respect by the mother. Slowly the child comes to regard the mother and other objects as entities apart from itself. One factor in this process is the neurological and the general physical development of the child, its ability to grasp objects—physically and mentally—and to master them. Through its own activity it experiences a world outside of itself. The process of individuation is furthered by that of education. This process entails a number of frustrations and prohibitions, which change the role of the mother into that of a person with different aims which conflict with the child's wishes, and often into that of a hostile and dangerous person. This antagonism, which is one part of the educational process though by no means the whole, is an important factor in sharpening the distinction between the "I" and the "thou."

A few months elapse after birth before the child even recognizes another person as such and is able to react with a smile, and it is years before the child ceases to confuse itself with the universe. Until then it shows the particular kind of egocentricity typical of children, an egocentricity which does not exclude tenderness for and interest in others, since "others" are not yet definitely experienced as really separate from itself. For the same reason the child's leaning on authority in these first years has also a different meaning from the leaning on authority later on. The parents, or whoever the authority may be, are not yet regarded as being a fundamentally separate entity; they are part of the child's universe, and this universe is still part of the child; submission to them, therefore, has a different quality from the kind of submission that exists once two individuals have become really separate. [. . .]

The more the child grows and to the extent to which primary ties are cut off, the more it develops a quest for freedom and independence. But the fate of this quest can only be fully understood if we realize the dialectic quality in this process of growing individuation.

This process has two aspects: One is that the child grows stronger physically, emotionally, and mentally. In each of these spheres intensity and activity grow. At the same time, these spheres become more and more integrated. An organized structure guided by the individual's will and reason develops. If we call this organized and integrated whole of the personality the self, we can also say that the *one side of the growing process of individuation is the growth of self-strength*. The limits of the growth of individuation and the self are set, partly by individual conditions, but essentially by social conditions. For although the differences between individuals in this respect appear to be great, every society is characterized by a certain level of individuation beyond which the normal individual cannot go.

The other aspect of the process of individuation is *growing aloneness*. The primary ties offer security and basic unity with the world outside of oneself. To the extent to which the child emerges from that world it becomes aware of being alone, of being an entity separate from all others. This separation from a world, which in comparison with one's own individual existence is overwhelmingly strong and powerful, and often threatening and dangerous, creates a feeling of powerlessness and anxiety. As long as one was an integral part of that world, unaware of the possibilities and responsibilities of individual action, one did not need to be afraid of it. When one has become an individual, one stands alone and faces the world in all its perilous and overpowering aspects.

Impulses arise to give up one's individuality, to overcome the feeling of aloneness and powerlessness by completely submerging oneself in the world outside. These impulses, however, and the new ties arising from them, are not identical with the primary ties which have been cut off in the process of growth itself. Just as a child can never return to the mother's womb physically, so it can never reverse, psychically, the process of individuation. Attempts to do so necessarily assume the character of submission, in which the basic contradiction between the authority and the child who submits to it is never eliminated. Consciously the child may feel secure and satisfied, but unconsciously it realizes that the price it pays is giving up strength and the integrity of its self. Thus the result of submission is the very opposite of what it was to be: Submission increases the child's insecurity and at the same time creates hostility and rebelliousness, which is the more frightening since it is directed against the very persons on whom the child has remained—or become—dependent.

However, submission is not the only way of avoiding aloneness and anxiety. The other way, the only one which is productive and does not end in an insoluble conflict, is that of *spontaneous relationship to man and nature*, a relationship that connects the individual with the world without eliminating his individuality. This kind of relationship—the foremost expressions of which are love and productive work—is rooted in the integration and strength of the total personality and is therefore subject to the very limits that exist for the growth of the self. [. . .]

I wish to point to the general principle, the dialectic process which results from growing individuation and from growing freedom of the individual. The child becomes more free *to* develop and express its own individual self unhampered by those ties which were limiting it. But the child also becomes more free *from* a world which gave it security and reassurance. The process of individuation is one of growing strength and integration of its individual personality, but it is at the same time a process in which the original identity with others is lost and in which the child becomes more separate from them. This growing separation may result in an isolation that has the quality of desolation and creates intense anxiety and insecurity; it may result in a new kind of closeness and a solidarity with others if the child has been able to develop the inner strength and productivity which are the premise of this new kind of relatedness to the world.

If every step in the direction of separation and individuation were matched by corresponding growth of the self, the development of the child would be harmonious. This does not occur, however. While the process of individuation takes place automatically, the growth of the self is hampered for a number of individual and social reasons. The lag between these two trends results in an unbearable feeling of isolation and powerlessness, and this in its turn leads to psychic *mechanisms of escape*.

Phylogenetically, too, the history of man can be characterized as a process of growing individuation and growing freedom. Man emerges from the prehuman stage by the first steps in the direction of becoming free from coercive instincts. If we understand by instinct a specific action pattern which is determined by inherited neurological structures, a clear-cut trend can be observed in the animal kingdom. (This concept of instinct should not be confused with one which speaks of instinct as a physiologically conditioned urge (such as hunger, thirst, and so on), the satisfaction of which occurs in ways which in themselves are not fixed and hereditarily determined.) The lower an animal is in the scale of development, the more are its adaptation to nature and all its activities controlled by instinctive and reflex action mechanisms. The famous social organizations of some insects are created entirely by instincts. On the other hand, the higher an animal is in the scale of development, the more flexibility of action pattern and the less completeness of structural adjustment do we find at birth. This development reaches its peak with man. He is the most helpless of all animals at birth. His adaptation to nature is based essentially on the process of learning, not on instinctual determination. "Instinct . . . is a diminishing if not a disappearing category in higher animal forms, especially in the human."[1]

Human existence begins when the lack of fixation of action by instincts exceeds a certain point; when the adaptation to nature loses its coercive character; when the way to act is no longer fixed by hereditarily given mechanisms. In other words, *human existence and freedom are from the beginning inseparable.* Freedom is here used not in its positive sense of "freedom to" but in its negative sense of "freedom from," namely freedom from instinctual determination of his actions.

Freedom in the sense just discussed is an ambiguous gift. Man is born without the equipment for appropriate action which the animal possesses;[2] he is dependent on his parents for a longer time than any animal, and his reactions to his surroundings are less quick and less effective than the automatically regulated instinctive actions are. He goes through all the dangers and fears which this lack of instinctive equipment implies. Yet this very helplessness of man is the basis from which human development springs; *man's biological weakness is the condition of human culture.*

From the beginning of his existence man is confronted with the choice between different courses of action. In the animal there is an uninterrupted chain of reactions starting with a stimulus, like hunger, and ending with a more or less strictly determined course of action, which does away with the tension created by the stimulus. In man that chain is interrupted. The stimulus is there but the kind of satisfaction is "open," that is, he must choose between different courses of action. Instead of a predetermined instinctive action, man has to weigh possible courses of action in his mind; he starts to think. He changes his role toward nature from that of purely passive adaptation to an active one: He produces. He invents tools and, while thus mastering nature, he separates himself from it more and more. He becomes dimly aware of himself—or rather of his group—as not being identical with nature. It dawns upon him that his is a tragic fate: to be part of nature, and yet to transcend it. He becomes aware of death as his ultimate fate even if he tries to deny it in manifold fantasies.

One particularly telling representation of the fundamental relation between man and freedom is offered in the biblical myth of man's expulsion from paradise.

1. L. Bernard, *Instinct* (New York: Holt & Co., 1924), 509.
2. Ralph Linton, *The Study of Man* (New York: D. Appleton-Century Company, 1936), ch. 4.

The myth identifies the beginning of human history with an act of choice, but it puts all emphasis on the sinfulness of this first act of freedom and the suffering resulting from it. Man and woman live in the Garden of Eden in complete harmony with each other and with nature. There is peace and no necessity to work; there is no choice, no freedom, no thinking either. Man is forbidden to eat from the tree of knowledge of good and evil. He acts against God's command, he breaks through the state of harmony with nature of which he is a part without transcending it. From the standpoint of the church, which represented authority, this is essentially sin. From the standpoint of man, however, this is the beginning of human freedom. Acting against God's orders means freeing himself from coercion, emerging from the unconscious existence of prehuman life to the level of man. Acting against the command of authority, committing a sin, is in its positive human aspect the first act of freedom, that is, the first *human* act. In the myth the sin in its formal aspect is the acting against God's command; in its material aspect it is the eating of the tree of knowledge. The act of disobedience as an act of freedom is the beginning of reason. The myth speaks of other consequences of the first act of freedom. The original harmony between man and nature is broken. God proclaims war between man and woman, and war between nature and man. Man has become separate from nature, he has taken the first step toward becoming human by becoming an "individual." He has committed the first act of freedom. The myth emphasizes the suffering resulting from this act. To transcend nature, to be alienated from nature and from another human being, finds man naked, ashamed. He is alone and free, yet powerless and afraid. The newly won freedom appears as a curse; he is free *from* the sweet bondage of paradise, but he is not free *to* govern himself, to realize his individuality.

"Freedom from" is not identical with positive freedom, with "freedom to." The emergence of man from nature is a long, drawn-out process; to a large extent he remains tied to the world from which he emerged; he remains part of nature—the soil he lives on, the sun and moon and stars, the trees and flowers, the animals, and the group of people with whom he is connected by the ties of blood. Primitive religions bear testimony to man's feeling of oneness with nature. Animate and inanimate nature are part of his human world or, as one may also put it, he is still part of the natural world.

These primary ties block his full human development; they stand in the way of the development of his reason and his critical capacities; they let him recognize himself and others only through the medium of his, or their, participation in a clan, a social or religious community, and not as human beings; in other words, they block his development as a free, self-determining, productive individual. But although this is one aspect, there is another one. This identity with nature, clan, religion, gives the individual security. He belongs to, he is rooted in, a structuralized whole in which he has an unquestionable place. He may suffer from hunger or suppression, but he does not suffer from the worst of all pains—complete aloneness and doubt.

We see that the process of growing human freedom has the same dialectic character that we have noticed in the process of individual growth. On the one hand it is a process of growing strength and integration, mastery of nature, growing power of human reason, and growing solidarity with other human beings. But on the other hand this growing individuation means growing isolation, insecurity, and thereby growing doubt concerning one's own role in the universe, the meaning of one's life, and with all that a growing feeling of one's own powerlessness and insignificance as an individual.

If the process of the development of mankind had been harmonious, if it had followed a certain plan, then both sides of the development—the growing strength and the growing individuation—would have been exactly balanced. As it is, the history of mankind is one of conflict and strife. Each step in the direction of growing individuation threatened people with new insecurities. Primary bonds once severed cannot be mended; once paradise is lost, man cannot return to it. There is only one possible, productive solution for the relationship of individualized man with the world: his active solidarity with all men and his spontaneous activity, love, and work, which unite him again with the world, not by primary ties but as a free and independent individual.

However, if the economic, social, and political conditions on which the whole process of human individuation depends do not offer a basis for the realization of individuality in the sense just mentioned, while at the same time people have lost those ties which gave them security, this lag makes freedom an unbearable burden. It then becomes identical with doubt, with a kind of life which lacks meaning and direction. Powerful tendencies arise to escape from this kind of freedom into submission or some kind of relationship to man and the world which promises relief from uncertainty, even if it deprives the individual of his freedom.

15

The Art of Loving

The desire for interpersonal fusion is the most powerful striving in man. It is the most fundamental passion, it is the force which keeps the human race together, the clan, the family, society. The failure to achieve it means insanity or destruction—self-destruction or destruction of others. Without love, humanity could not exist for a day. Yet, if we call the achievement of interpersonal union "love," we find ourselves in a serious difficulty. Fusion can be achieved in different ways—and the differences are not less significant than what is common to the various forms of love. Should they all be called love? Or should we reserve the word *love* only for a specific kind of union, one which has been the ideal virtue in all great humanistic religions and philosophical systems of the last four thousand years of Western and Eastern history?

As with all semantic difficulties, the answer can only be arbitrary. What matters is that we know what kind of union we are talking about when we speak of love. Do we refer to love as the mature answer to the problem of existence, or do we speak of those immature forms of love which may be called *symbiotic union*? In the following pages I shall call love only the former. I shall begin the discussion of "love" with the latter.

Symbiotic union has its biological pattern in the relationship between the pregnant mother and the fetus. They are two, and yet one. They live "together" (*sym-biosis*), they need each other. The fetus is a part of the mother, it receives everything it needs from her; mother is its world, as it were; she feeds it, she protects it, but also her own life is enhanced by it. In the *psychic* symbiotic union, the two bodies are independent, but the same kind of attachment exists psychologically.

The *passive* form of the symbiotic union is that of submission, or if we use a clinical term, of *masochism*. The masochistic person escapes from the unbearable feeling of isolation and separateness by making himself part and parcel of another person who directs him, guides him, protects him; who is his life and his oxygen, as it were. The power of the one to whom one submits is inflated, may he be a person or a god; he is everything, I am nothing, except inasmuch as I am part of him. As a part, I am part of greatness, of power, of certainty. The masochistic person does not have to make decisions, does not have to take any risks; he is never alone—but he is not independent; he has no integrity; he is not yet fully born. In a religious context the object of worship is called an idol; in a secular context of a masochistic love relationship the essential mechanism, that of idolatry, is the same. The masochistic relationship can be blended with physical, sexual desire; in this case it is not only a submission in which one's mind participates, but also one's whole body. There can be masochistic submission to fate, to sickness, to rhythmic music, to the orgiastic state produced by drugs or under hypnotic trance—in all these instances the person renounces his integrity, makes himself the instrument of somebody or something outside of himself; he need not solve the problem of living by productive activity.

The *active* form of symbiotic fusion is domination or, to use the psychological term corresponding to masochism, *sadism*. The sadistic person wants to escape from his aloneness and his sense of imprisonment by making another person part and parcel of himself. He inflates and enhances himself by incorporating another person, who worships him.

The sadistic person is as dependent on the submissive person as the latter is on the former; neither can live without the other. The difference is only that the sadistic person commands, exploits, hurts, humiliates, and that the masochistic person is commanded, exploited, hurt, humiliated. This is a considerable difference in a realistic sense; in a deeper emotional sense, the difference is not so great as that which they both have in common: fusion without integrity. If one understands this, it is also not surprising to find that usually a person reacts in both the sadistic and the masochistic manner, usually toward different objects. [. . .]

In contrast to symbiotic union, mature *love* is *union under the condition of preserving one's integrity*, one's individuality. *Love is an active power in man*; a power which breaks through the walls which separate man from his fellow men, which unites him with others; love makes him overcome the sense of isolation and separateness, yet it permits him to be himself, to retain his integrity. In love the paradox occurs that two beings become one and yet remain two. [. . .]

Love is an activity, not a passive affect; it is a "standing in," not a "falling for." In the most general way, the active character of love can be described by stating that love is primarily *giving*, not receiving. [...]

What does one person give to another? He gives of himself, of the most precious he has, he gives of his life. This does not necessarily mean that he sacrifices his life for the other—but that he gives him of that which is alive in him; he gives him of his joy, of his interest, of his understanding, of his knowledge, of his humor, of his sadness—of all expressions and manifestations of that which is alive in him. In thus giving of his life, he enriches the other person, he enhances the other's sense of aliveness by enhancing his own sense of aliveness. He does not give in order to receive; giving is in itself exquisite joy. But in giving he cannot help bringing something to life in the other person, and this which is brought to life reflects back to him; in truly giving, he cannot help receiving that which is given back to him. Giving implies to make the other person a giver also and they both share in the joy of what they have brought to life. In the act of giving something is born, and both persons involved are grateful for the life that is born for both of them. Specifically with regard to love this means: Love is a power which produces love; impotence is the inability to produce love. This thought has been beautifully expressed by Marx:

> Assume *man* as *man*, and his relation to the world as a human one, and you can exchange love only for love, confidence for confidence, etc. If you wish to enjoy art, you must be an artistically trained person; if you wish to have influence on other people, you must be a person who has a really stimulating and furthering influence on other people. Every one of your relationships to man and to nature must be a definite expression of your *real, individual* life corresponding to the object of your will. If you love without calling forth love, that is, if your love as such does not produce love, if by means of an *expression of life* as a loving person you do not make of yourself a *loved person*, then your love is impotent, a misfortune.[1]

But not only in love does giving mean receiving. The teacher is taught by his students, the actor is stimulated by his audience, the psychoanalyst is cured by his patient—provided they do not treat each other as objects, but are related to each other genuinely and productively.

It is hardly necessary to stress the fact that the ability to love as an act of giving depends on the character development of the person. It presupposes the attainment of a predominantly productive orientation; in this orientation the person has overcome dependency, narcissistic omnipotence, the wish to exploit others, or to hoard, and has acquired faith in his own human powers, courage to rely on his powers in the attainment of his goals.

1. Karl Marx, "Nationalökonomie und Philosophie" (1844), in Karl Marx, *Die Frühschriften* (Stuttgart: Alfred Kröner Verlag, 1953), 300, 301. (My translation—E. F.)

16

Self-Love, Selfishness, Selflessness

The doctrine that selfishness is the arch-evil and that to love oneself excludes loving others is by no means restricted to theology and philosophy, but it became one of the stock ideas promulgated in home, school, motion pictures, books; indeed in all instruments of social suggestion as well. "Don't be selfish" is a sentence which has been impressed upon millions of children, generation after generation. Its meaning is somewhat vague. Most people would say that it means not to be egotistical, inconsiderate, without any concern for others. Actually, it generally means more than that. Not to be selfish implies not to do what one wishes, to give up one's own wishes for the sake of those in authority. "Don't be selfish," in the last analysis, has the same ambiguity that it has in Calvinism. Aside from its obvious implication, it means, "don't love yourself," "don't be yourself," but submit yourself to something more important than yourself, to an outside power or its internalization, "duty." "Don't be selfish" becomes one of the most powerful ideological tools in suppressing spontaneity and the free development of personality. Under the pressure of this slogan one is asked for every sacrifice and for complete submission: Only those acts are "unselfish" which do not serve the individual but somebody or something outside himself.

This picture, we must repeat, is in a certain sense one-sided. For besides the doctrine that one should not be selfish, the opposite is also propagandized in modern society: Keep your own advantage in mind, act according to what is best for you; by so doing you will also be acting for the greatest advantage of all others. As a matter of fact, the idea that egotism is the basis of the general welfare is the principle on which competitive society has been built. It is puzzling that two such seemingly contradictory principles could be taught side by side in one culture; of the fact, however, there is no doubt. One result of this contradiction is confusion in the individual. Torn between the two doctrines, he is seriously blocked in the process of integrating his personality. This confusion is one of the most significant sources of the bewilderment and helplessness of modern man.

The doctrine that love for oneself is identical with "selfishness" and an alternative to love for others has pervaded theology, philosophy, and popular thought; the same doctrine has been rationalized in scientific language in *Freud's* theory of narcissism. Freud's concept presupposes a fixed amount of libido. In the infant, all of the libido has the child's own person as its objective, the stage of "primary narcissism," as Freud calls it. During the individual's development, the libido is shifted from one's own person toward other objects. If a person is blocked in his "object-relationships," the libido is withdrawn from the objects and returned to his own person; this is called "secondary narcissism." According to Freud, the more love I turn toward the outside world the less love is left for myself, and vice versa. He thus describes the phenomenon of love as an impoverishment of one's self-love because all libido is turned to an object outside oneself.

These questions arise: Does psychological observation support the thesis that there is a basic contradiction and a state of alternation between love for oneself and love for others? Is love for oneself the same phenomenon as selfishness, or are they opposites? Furthermore, is the selfishness of modern man really a *concern for himself* as an individual, with all his intellectual, emotional, and sensual potentialities? Has "he" not become an appendage of his socioeconomic role? *Is his selfishness identical with self-love or is it not caused by the very lack of it?*

Before we start the discussion of the psychological aspect of selfishness and self-love, the logical fallacy in the notion that love for others and love for oneself are mutually exclusive should be stressed. If it is a virtue to love my neighbor as a human being, it must be a virtue—and not a vice— to love myself since I am a human being too. There is no concept of man in which I myself am not included. A doctrine which proclaims such an exclusion proves itself to be intrinsically contradictory. The idea expressed in the biblical "Love thy neighbor as thyself!" implies that respect for one's own integrity and uniqueness, love for and understanding of one's own self, cannot be separated from respect for and love and understanding of another individual. The love for my own self is inseparably connected with the love for any other self.

We have come now to the basic psychological premises on which the conclusions of our argument are built. Generally, these premises are as follows: Not only others, but we ourselves are the "object" of our feelings and attitudes; the attitudes toward others and toward ourselves, far from being contradictory, are basically *conjunctive*. With regard to the problem under discussion this means: Love of others and love of ourselves are not alternatives. On the contrary, an attitude of love toward themselves will be found in all those who are capable of loving others. *Love*, in principle, *is indivisible as far as the connection between "objects" and one's own self is concerned*. Genuine love is an expression of productiveness and implies care, respect, responsibility, and knowledge. It is not an "affect" in the sense of being affected by somebody, but an active striving for the growth and happiness of the loved person, rooted in one's own capacity to love.

To love is an expression of one's power to love, and to love somebody is the actualization and concentration of this power with regard to one person. It is not true, as the idea of romantic love would have it, that there is only *the* one person in the world whom one could love and that it is the great chance of one's life to find that one person. Nor is it true, if that person be found that love for him (or her) results in a withdrawal of love from others. Love which can only be experienced with regard to one person demonstrates by this very fact that it is not love, but a symbiotic attachment. The basic affirmation contained in love is directed toward the beloved person as an incarnation of essentially human qualities. Love of one person implies love of man as such. The kind of "division of labor" as William James calls it, by which one loves one's family but is without feeling for the "stranger," is a sign of a basic inability to love. Love of man is not, as is frequently supposed, an abstraction coming after the love for a specific person, but it is its premise, although, genetically, it is acquired in loving specific individuals.

From this it follows that my own self, in principle, must be as much an object of my love as another person. *The affirmation of one's own life, happiness, growth, freedom, is rooted in one's capacity to love*, i.e., in care, respect, responsibility, and knowledge. If an individual is able to love productively, he loves himself too; if he can love *only* others, he cannot love at all.

Granted that love for oneself and for others in principle is conjunctive, how do we explain selfishness, which obviously excludes any genuine concern for others? The *selfish* person is interested only in himself, wants everything for himself, feels no pleasure in giving, but only in taking. The world outside is looked at only from the standpoint of what he can get out of it; he lacks interest in the needs of others, and respect for their dignity and integrity. He can see nothing but himself; he judges everyone and everything from its usefulness to him; he is basically unable to love.

Does not this prove that concern for others and concern for oneself are unavoidable alternatives? This would be so if selfishness and self-love were identical. But that assumption is the very fallacy which has led to so many mistaken conclusions concerning our problem. *Selfishness and self-love, far from being identical, are actually opposites.* The selfish person does not love himself too much but too little; in fact he hates himself. This lack of fondness and care for himself, which is only one expression of his lack of productiveness, leaves him empty and frustrated. He is necessarily unhappy and anxiously concerned to snatch from life the satisfactions which he blocks himself from attaining. He seems to care too much for himself but actually he only makes an unsuccessful attempt to cover up and compensate for his failure to care for his real self. Freud holds that the selfish person is narcissistic, as if he had withdrawn his love from others and turned it toward his own person. *It is true that selfish persons are incapable of loving others, but they are not capable of loving themselves either.*

It is easier to understand selfishness by comparing it with greedy concern for others, as we find it, for instance, in an oversolicitous, dominating mother. While she consciously believes that she is particularly fond of her child, she has actually a deeply repressed hostility toward the object of her concern. She is overconcerned not because she loves the child too much, but because she has to compensate for her lack of capacity to love him at all.

This theory of the nature of selfishness is borne out by psychoanalytic experience with neurotic "unselfishness," a symptom of neurosis observed in not a few people who usually are troubled not by this symptom but by others connected with it, like depression, tiredness, inability to work, failure in love relationships, and so on. Not only is unselfishness not felt as a "symptom"; it is often the one redeeming character trait on which such people pride themselves. The "unselfish" person "does not want anything for himself"; he "lives only for others," is proud that he does not consider himself important. He is puzzled to find that in spite of his unselfishness he is unhappy, and that his relationships to those closest to him are unsatisfactory. He wants to have what he considers are his symptoms removed—but not his unselfishness. Analytic work shows that his unselfishness is not something apart from his other symptoms but one of them; in fact often the most important one; that he is paralyzed in his capacity to love or to enjoy anything; that he is pervaded by hostility against life and that behind the facade of unselfishness a subtle but no less intense self-centeredness is hidden. This person can be cured only if his unselfishness too is interpreted as a symptom along with the others so that his lack of productiveness, which is at the root of both his unselfishness *and* his other troubles, can be corrected.

The nature of unselfishness becomes particularly apparent in its effect on others and most frequently, in our culture, in the effect the "unselfish" mother has on her children. She believes that by her unselfishness her children will experience what it means to be loved and to learn, in turn, what it means to love. The effect of her unselfishness, however, does not at all correspond to her expectations. The children do not show the happiness of persons who are convinced that they are loved; they are anxious, tense, afraid of the mother's disapproval and anxious to live up to her expectations. Usually, they are affected by their mother's hidden hostility against life, which they sense rather than recognize, and eventually become imbued with it themselves. Altogether, the effect of the "unselfish" mother is not too different from that of the selfish one; indeed, it is often worse because the mother's unselfishness prevents the children from criticizing her. They are put under the obligation not to disappoint her; they are taught, under the mask of virtue, dislike for life. If one has a chance to study the effect of a mother with genuine self-love, one can see that there is nothing more conducive to giving a child the experience of what love, joy, and happiness are than being loved by a mother who loves herself.

PART VI

Faith in Humanity

Fromm's growing interest in psychoanalysis led him to break with Orthodox Judaism in the 1920s. His experience of a "spiritual dimension" with the lifting of repression in psychoanalysis proved strong enough to sweep aside traditional religious notions of a personal God. After his rejection of religion, Fromm may have had strong atheistic leanings for many years, but if this was the case, he never expressed them. In his view, arguing for or against the existence of God was a waste of energies that could be better devoted to human concerns and the experience of *humanitas*.

Fromm is a humanist in the narrow sense of the word: The origin and goal of all human reality is man himself; the only path is a human one. Redemption is liberation to existence as a full human being, to a higher self, to *humanitas*. God is a symbol for the aims of a humane development, and the experience of God is the experience of man's higher self. It is a mystical experience of oneness, in which man and the idea of God are freed from all need to "have." The humanistic creed distinguishes between humanistic and authoritarian religions (see *Psychoanalysis and Religion* [1950]); the humanistic creed acknowledges religious experience and the experience of God, but without the concept of God (as described in *You Shall Be as God* [1966]); the humanistic creed professes all religious values in which there is mystical experience of oneness: in Zen Buddhism, as Fromm learned it from Daisetz T. Suzuki in the 1950s; in the Buddhist mysticism Fromm learned of at the end of his life through Nyanaponika Mahathera; in the form of Islamic mysticism known as Sufism and in Christian mysticism, particularly that of Meister Eckhart. Of course the origins of this humanistic credo lie in the Jewish mysticism of the Hasidim. Fromm remained a Hasid throughout his life.

17

The Humanistic Credo

I believe that man is the product of natural evolution; that he is part of nature and yet transcends it, being endowed with reason and self-awareness.

I believe that man's essence is ascertainable. However, this essence is not a substance which characterizes man at all times through history. The essence of man consists in the above-mentioned contradiction inherent in his existence, and this contradiction forces him to react in order to find a solution. Man cannot remain neutral and passive toward this existential dichotomy. By the very fact of his being human, he is asked a question by life: how to overcome the split between himself and the world outside of him in order to arrive at the experience of unity and oneness with his fellow man and with nature. Man has to answer this question every moment of his life. Not only—or even primarily—with thoughts and words, but by his mode of being and acting.

I believe that there are a number of limited and ascertainable answers to this question of existence (the history of religion and philosophy is a catalogue of these answers); yet there are basically only two categories of answers. In one, man attempts to find again harmony with nature by regression to a prehuman form of existence, eliminating his specifically human qualities of reason and love. In the other, his goal is the full development of his human powers until he reaches a new harmony with his fellow man and with nature.

I believe that the first answer is bound to failure. It leads to death, destruction, suffering, and never to the full growth of man, never to harmony and strength. The second answer requires the elimination of greed and egocentricity, it demands discipline, will, and respect for those who can show the way. Yet, although this answer is the more difficult one, it is the only answer which is not doomed to failure. In fact, even before the final goal is reached, the activity and effort expended in approaching it has a unifying and integrating effect which intensifies man's vital energies.

I believe that man's basic alternative is the choice between life and death. Every act implies this choice. Man is free to make it, but this freedom is a limited one. There are many favorable and unfavorable conditions which incline him—his psychological constitution, the condition of the specific society into which he was born, his family, teachers, and the friends he meets and chooses. It is man's task to enlarge the margin of freedom, to strengthen the conditions which are conducive to life as against those which are conducive to death. Life and death, as spoken of here, are not the biological states, but states of being, of relating to the world. Life means constant change, constant birth. Death means cessation of growth, ossification, repetition. The unhappy fate of many is that they do not make the choice. They are neither alive nor dead. Life becomes a burden, an aimless enterprise, and busyness is the means to protect one from the torture of being in the land of shadows.

I believe that neither life nor history has an ultimate meaning which in turn imparts meaning to the life of the individual or justifies his suffering. Considering the contradictions and weaknesses which beset man's existence, it is only too natural that he seeks for an "absolute" which gives him the illusion of certainty and relieves him from conflict, doubt, and responsibility. Yet, no god, neither in theological, philosophical, or historical garments, saves or condemns man. Only man can find a goal for life and the means for the realization of this goal. He cannot find a saving ultimate or absolute answer, but he can strive for a degree of intensity, depth, and clarity of experience which gives him the strength to live without illusions, and to be free.

I believe that no one can "save" his fellow man by making the choice for him. All that one man can do for another is to show him the alternatives truthfully and lovingly, yet without sentimentality or illusion. Confrontation with the true alternatives may awaken all the hidden energies in a person, and enable him to choose life as against death. If he cannot choose life, no one else can breathe life into him.

I believe that there are two ways of arriving at the choice of the good. The first is that of duty and obedience to moral commands. This way can be effective, yet one must consider that in thousands of years only a minority have fulfilled even the requirements of the Ten Commandments. Many more have committed crimes when they were presented to them as commands by those in authority. The other way is to develop a taste for and a sense of well-being in doing what is good or right. By taste for well-being, I do not mean pleasure in the Benthamian or Freudian sense. I refer to the sense of heightened aliveness in which I confirm my powers and my identity.

I believe that education means to acquaint the young with the best heritage of the human race. But while much of this heritage is expressed in words, it is effective only if these words become reality in the person of the teacher and in the practice and structure of society. Only the idea which has materialized in the flesh can influence man; the idea which remains a word only changes words.

I believe in the perfectibility of man. This perfectibility means that man *can* reach his goal, but it does not mean that he *must* reach it. If the individual will not choose life and does not grow, he will by necessity become destructive, a living corpse. Evilness and self-loss are as real as are goodness and aliveness. They are the secondary potentialities of man if he chooses not to realize his primary potentialities.

I believe that only exceptionally is a man born as a saint or as a criminal. Most of us have dispositions for good and for evil, although the respective weight of these dispositions varies with individuals. Hence, our fate is largely determined by those influences which mold and form the given dispositions. The family is the most important influence. But the family itself is mainly an agent of society, the transmission belt for those values and norms which a society wants to impress on its members. Hence, the most important factor for the development of the individual is the structure and the values of the society into which he has been born.

I believe that society has both a furthering and an inhibiting function. Only in cooperation with others, and in the process of work, does man develop his powers, only in the historical process does he create himself. But at the same time, most societies until now have served the aims of the few who wanted to use the many. Hence they had to use their power to stultify and intimidate the many (and thus, indirectly, themselves), to prevent them from developing all their powers; for this reason society has always conflicted with humanity, with the universal norms valid for every man. Only when society's aim will have become identical with the aims of humanity, will society cease to cripple man and to further evil.

I believe that every man represents humanity. We are different as to intelligence, health, talents. Yet we are all one. We are all saints and sinners, adults and children, and no one is anybody's superior or judge. We have all been awakened with the Buddha, we have all been crucified with Christ, and we have all killed and robbed with Genghis Khan, Stalin, and Hitler.

I believe that man can visualize the experience of the whole universal man only by realizing his individuality and never by trying to reduce himself to an abstract, common denominator. Man's task in life is precisely the paradoxical one of realizing his individuality and at the same time transcending it and arriving at the experience of universality. Only the fully developed individual self can drop the ego.

I believe that the One World which is emerging can come into existence only if a New Man comes into being—a man who has emerged from the archaic ties of blood and soil, and who feels himself to be the son of man, a citizen of the world whose loyalty is to the human race and to life, rather than to any exclusive part of it; a man who loves his country because he loves mankind, and whose judgment is not warped by tribal loyalties.

I believe that man's growth is a process of continuous birth, of continuous awakening. We are usually half-asleep and only sufficiently awake to go about our business; but we are not awake enough to go about living, which is the only task that matters for a living being. The great leaders of the human race are those who have awakened man from his half-slumber. The great enemies of humanity are those who put it to sleep, and it does not matter whether their sleeping potion is the worship of God or that of the golden calf.

I believe that the development of man in the last four thousand years of history is truly awe-inspiring. He has developed his reason to a point where he is solving the riddles of nature, and has emancipated himself from the blind power of the natural forces. But at the very moment of his greatest triumph, when he is at the threshold of a new world, he has succumbed to the power of the very things and organizations he has created. He has invented a new method of producing, and has made production and distribution his new idol. He worships the work of his hands and has reduced himself to being the servant of things. He uses the name of God, of freedom, of humanity, of socialism, in vain; he prides himself on his powers—the bombs and the machines—to cover up his human bankruptcy; he boasts of his power to destroy in order to hide his human impotence.

I believe that the only force that can save us from self-destruction is reason; the capacity to recognize the unreality of most of the ideas that man holds, and to penetrate to the reality veiled by the layers and layers of deception and ideologies; reason, not as a body of knowledge, but as a "kind of energy, a force which is fully comprehensible only in its agency and effects..." a force whose "most important function consists in its power to bind and to dissolve."[1] Violence and arms will not save us; sanity and reason may.

---

1. Ernst Cassirer, *The Philosophy of the Enlightenment* (Boston: Beacon Press, 1955), 13.

I believe that reason cannot be effective unless man has hope and belief. Goethe was right when he said that the deepest distinction between various historical periods is that between belief and disbelief, and when he added that all epochs in which belief dominates are brilliant, uplifting, and fruitful, while those in which disbelief dominates vanish because nobody cares to devote himself to the unfruitful. No doubt the thirteenth century, the Renaissance, the Enlightenment, were ages of belief and hope. I am afraid that the Western world in the twentieth century deceives itself about the fact that it has lost hope and belief. Truly, where there is no belief in man, the belief in machines will not save us from vanishing; on the contrary, this "belief" will only accelerate the end. Either the Western world will be capable of creating a renaissance of humanism in which the fullest developments of man's humanity, and not production and work, are the central issues—or the West will perish as many other great civilizations have.

I believe that to recognize the truth is not primarily a matter of intelligence, but a matter of character. The most important element is the courage to say *no*, to disobey the commands of power and of public opinion; to cease being asleep and to become human; to wake up and lose the sense of helplessness and futility. Eve and Prometheus are the two great rebels whose very "crimes" liberated mankind. But the capacity to say "no" meaningfully, implies the capacity to say "yes" meaningfully. The "yes" to God is the "no" to Caesar; the "yes" to man is the "no" to all those who want to enslave, exploit, and stultify him.

I believe in freedom, in man's right to be himself, to assert himself and to fight all those who try to prevent him from being himself. But freedom is more than the absence of violent oppression. It is more than "freedom from." It is "freedom to"—the freedom to become independent; the freedom to *be* much, rather than to *have* much, or to *use* things and people.

I believe that neither Western capitalism nor Soviet or Chinese communism can solve the problem of the future. They both create bureaucracies which transform man into a thing. Man must bring the forces of nature and of society under his conscious and rational control; but not under the control of a bureaucracy which administers things *and* man, but under the control of the free and associated producers who administer things and subordinate them to man, who is the measure of all things. The alternative is not between "capitalism" and "communism" but between bureaucratism and humanism. Democratic, decentralizing socialism is the realization of those conditions which are necessary to make the unfolding of all man's powers the ultimate purpose.

I believe that one of the most disastrous mistakes in individual and social life consists in being caught in stereotyped alternatives of thinking.

"Better dead than Red," "an alienated industrial civilization or individualistic preindustrial society," "to rearm or to be helpless," are examples of such alternatives. There are always other and new possibilities which become apparent only when one has liberated oneself from the deathly grip of clichés, and when one permits the voice of humanity, and reason, to be heard. The principle of "the lesser evil" is the principle of despair. Most of the time it only lengthens the period until the greater evil wins out. To risk doing what is right and human, and have faith in the power of the voice of humanity and truth, is more realistic than the so-called realism of opportunism.

I believe that man must get rid of illusions that enslave and paralyze him; that he must become aware of the reality inside and outside of him in order to create a world which needs no illusions. Freedom and independence can be achieved only when the chains of illusion are broken.

I believe that today there is only one main concern: the question of war and peace. Man is likely to destroy all life on earth, or to destroy all civilized life and the values among those that remain, and to build a barbaric, totalitarian organization which will rule what is left of mankind. To wake up to this danger, to look through the double talk on all sides which is used to prevent men from seeing the abyss toward which they are moving is the one obligation, the one moral and intellectual command which man must respect today. If he does not, we all will be doomed.

If we should all perish in the nuclear holocaust, it will not be because man was not capable of becoming human, or that he was inherently evil; it would be because the consensus of stupidity has prevented him from seeing reality and acting upon the truth.

I believe in the perfectibility of man, but I doubt whether he will achieve this goal, unless he awakens soon.

> Watchman, what of the night?
> The watchman says:
> Morning comes and also the night
> If you will inquire, inquire:
> Return, come back again.

> Isaiah 21

18

Authoritarian versus Humanistic Religion

What is the principle of authoritarian religion? The definition of religion given in the *Oxford Dictionary*, while attempting to define religion as such, is a rather accurate definition of authoritarian religion. It reads: "[Religion is] recognition on the part of man of some higher unseen power as having control of his destiny, and as being entitled to obedience, reverence, and worship."

Here the emphasis is on the recognition that man is controlled by a higher power outside of himself. But this alone does not constitute authoritarian religion. What makes it so is the idea that this power, because of the control it exercises, is *entitled* to "obedience, reverence, and worship." I italicize the word *entitled* because it shows that the reason for worship, obedience, and reverence lies not in the moral qualities of the deity, not in love or justice, but in the fact that it has control, that is, has power over man. Furthermore it shows that the higher power has a right to force man to worship him and that lack of reverence and obedience constitutes sin.

The essential element in authoritarian religion and in the authoritarian religious experience is the surrender to a power transcending man. The main virtue of this type of religion is obedience, its cardinal sin is disobedience. Just as the deity is conceived as omnipotent or omniscient, man is conceived as being powerless and insignificant. Only as he can gain grace or help from the deity by complete surrender can he feel strength. Submission to a powerful authority is one of the avenues by which man escapes from his feeling of aloneness and limitation. In the act of surrender he loses his independence and integrity as an individual but he gains the feeling of being protected by an awe-inspiring power of which, as it were, he becomes a part.

From *Psychoanalysis and Religion* by Erich Fromm (New Haven: Yale University Press, 1950). Copyright © 1950 by Erich Fromm. Reprinted by permission of Yale University Press.

In Calvin's theology we find a vivid picture of authoritarian, theistic thinking:

> For I do not call it humility, if you suppose that we have anything left. . . . We cannot think of ourselves as we ought to think without utterly despising everything that may be supposed an excellence in us. This humility is unfeigned submission of a mind overwhelmed with a weighty sense of its own misery and poverty; for such is the uniform description of it in the word of God.[1]

The experience which Calvin describes here, that of despising everything in oneself, of the submission of the mind overwhelmed by its own poverty, is the very essence of all authoritarian religions whether they are couched in secular or in theological language. In authoritarian religion God is a symbol of power and force, He is supreme because He has supreme power, and man in juxtaposition is utterly powerless.

Authoritarian secular religion follows the same principle. Here the führer or the beloved "father of his people" or the state or the race or the socialist fatherland becomes the object of worship; the life of the individual becomes insignificant and man's worth consists in the very denial of his worth and strength. Frequently authoritarian religion postulates an ideal which is so abstract and so distant that it has hardly any connection with the real life of real people. To such ideals as "life after death" or "the future of mankind" the life and happiness of persons living here and now may be sacrificed; the alleged ends justify every means and become symbols in the names of which religious or secular "elites" control the lives of their fellow men.

Humanistic religion, on the contrary, is centered around man and his strength. Man must develop his power of reason in order to understand himself, his relationship to his fellow men, and his position in the universe. He must recognize the truth, both with regard to his limitations and his potentialities. He must develop his powers of love for others as well as for himself and experience the solidarity of all living beings. He must have principles and norms to guide him in this aim. Religious experience in this kind of religion is the experience of oneness with the all, based on one's relatedness to the world as it is grasped with thought and with love. Man's aim in humanistic religion is to achieve the greatest strength, not the greatest powerlessness; virtue is self-realization, not obedience. Faith is certainty of conviction based on one's experience of thought and feeling, not assent to propositions on credit of the proposer. The

---

1. Johannes Calvin, *Institutes of the Christian Religion* (Presbyterian Board of Christian Education, 1928), 681.

prevailing mood is that of joy, while the prevailing mood in authoritarian religion is that of sorrow and of guilt.

Inasmuch as humanistic religions are theistic, God is a symbol of *man's own powers* which he tries to realize in his life, and is not a symbol of force and domination, having *power over man.*

Illustrations of humanistic religions are early Buddhsim, Taoism, the teachings of Isaiah, Jesus, Socrates, Spinoza, certain trends in the Jewish and Christian religions (particularly mysticism), the religion of Reason of the French Revolution. It is evident from these that the distinction between authoritarian and humanistic religion cuts across the distinction between theistic and nontheistic, and between religions in the narrow sense of the word and philosophical systems of religious character. What matters in all such systems is not the thought system as such but the human attitude underlying their doctrines. [...]

While in humanistic religion God is the image of man's higher self, a symbol of what man potentially is or ought to become, in authoritarian religion God becomes the sole possessor of what was originally man's: of his reason and his love. The more perfect God becomes, the more imperfect becomes man. He *projects* the best he has onto God and thus impoverishes himself. Now God has all love, all wisdom, all justice—and man is deprived of these qualities, he is empty and poor. He had begun with the feeling of smallness, but he now has become completely powerless and without strength; all his powers have been projected onto God. This mechanism of projection is the very same which can be observed in interpersonal relationships of a masochistic, submissive character, where one person is awed by another and attributes his own powers and aspirations to the other person. It is the same mechanism that makes people endow the leaders of even the most inhuman systems with qualities of superwisdom and kindness.

When man has thus projected his own most valuable powers onto God, what of his relationship to his own powers? They have become separated from him and in this process he has become *alienated* from himself. Everything he has is now God's and nothing is left in him. *His only access to himself is through God.* In worshipping God he tries to get in touch with that part of himself which he has lost through projection. After having given God all he has, he begs God to return to him some of what originally was his own. But having lost his own he is completely at God's mercy. He necessarily feels like a "sinner" since he has deprived himself of everything that is good, and it is only through God's mercy or grace that he can regain that which alone makes him human. And in order to persuade God to give him some of his love, he must prove to him how utterly deprived he is of love; in order to persuade God to guide him by his superior wisdom he must prove to him how deprived he is of wisdom when he is left to himself.

But this alienation from his own powers not only makes man feel slavishly dependent on God, it makes him bad too. He becomes a man without faith in his fellow men or in himself, without the experience of his own love, of his own power of reason. As a result the separation between the "holy" and the "secular" occurs. In his worldly activities man acts without love, in that sector of his life which is reserved to religion he feels himself to be a sinner (which he actually is, since to live without love is to live in sin) and tries to recover some of his lost humanity by being in touch with God. Simultaneously, he tries to win forgiveness by emphasizing his own helplessness and worthlessness. Thus the attempt to obtain forgiveness results in the activation of the very attitude from which his sins stem. He is caught in a painful dilemma. The more he praises God, the emptier he becomes. The emptier he becomes, the more sinful he feels. The more sinful he feels, the more he praises his God—and the less able is he to regain himself.

Analysis of religion must not stop at uncovering those psychological processes within man which underlie his religious experience; it must proceed to discover the conditions which make for the development of authoritarian and humanistic character structures, respectively, from which different kinds of religious experience stem. Such a sociopsychological analysis goes far beyond the context of these chapters. However, the principal point can be made briefly. What people think and feel is rooted in their character and their character is molded by the total configuration of their practice of life—more precisely, by the socioeconomic and political structure of their society. In societies ruled by a powerful minority which holds the masses in subjection, the individual will be so imbued with fear, so incapable of feeling strong or independent, that his religious experience will be authoritarian. Whether he worships a punishing, awesome God or a similarly conceived leader makes little difference. On the other hand, where the individual feels free and responsible for his own fate, or among minorities striving for freedom and independence, humanistic religious experience develops. The history of religion gives ample evidence of this correlation between social structure and kinds of religious experience. Early Christianity was a religion of the poor and downtrodden; the history of religious sects fighting against authoritarian political pressure shows the same principle again and again. Judaism, in which a strong anti-authoritarian tradition could grow up because secular authority never had much of a chance to govern and to build up a legend of its wisdom, therefore developed the humanistic aspect of religion to a remarkable degree. Whenever, on the other hand, religion allied itself with secular power, the religion had by necessity to become authoritarian. The real fall of man is his alienation from himself, his submission to power, his turning against himself even though under the guise of his worship of God.

From the spirit of authoritarian religion stem two fallacies of reasoning which have been used again and again as arguments for theistic religion. One argument runs as follows: How can you criticize the emphasis on dependence on a power transcending man; is not man dependent on forces outside himself which he cannot understand, much less control?

Indeed, man is dependent; he remains subject to death, age, illness, and even if he were to control nature and to make it wholly serviceable to him, he and his earth remain tiny specks in the universe. But it is one thing to recognize one's dependence and limitations, and it is something entirely different to indulge in this dependence, to worship the forces on which one depends. To understand realistically and soberly how limited our power is is an essential part of wisdom and of maturity; to worship it is masochistic and self-destructive. The one is humility, the other self-humiliation.

We can study the difference between the realistic recognition of our limitations and the indulgence in the experience of submission and powerlessness in the clinical examination of masochistic character traits. We find people who have a tendency to incur sickness, accidents, humiliating situations, who belittle and weaken themselves. They believe that they get into such situations against their will and intention, but a study of their unconscious motives shows that actually they are driven by one of the most irrational tendencies to be found in man, namely, by an unconscious desire to be weak and powerless; they tend to shift the center of their life to powers over which they feel no control, thus escaping from freedom and from personal responsibility. We find furthermore that this masochistic tendency is usually accompanied by its very opposite, the tendency to rule and to dominate others, and that the masochistic and the dominating tendencies form the two sides of the authoritarian character structure. Such masochistic tendencies are not always unconscious. We find them overtly in the sexual masochistic perversion where the fulfillment of the wish to be hurt or humiliated is the condition for sexual excitement and satisfaction. We find it also in the relationship to the leader and the state in all authoritarian secular religions. Here the explicit aim is to give up one's own will and to experience submission under the leader or the state as profoundly rewarding.

Another fallacy of theological thinking is closely related to the one concerning dependence. I mean here the argument that there must be a power or being outside of man because we find that man has an ineradicable longing to relate himself to something beyond himself. Indeed, any sane human being has a need to relate himself to others; a person who has lost that capacity completely is insane. No wonder that man has created figures outside of himself to which he relates himself, which he loves and cherishes because they are not subject to the vacillations and inconsistencies of human objects. That God is a symbol of man's need to love is simple enough to understand. But does it follow from the existence and intensity of this human need that there exists an outer being who corresponds to this need? Obviously that follows as little as our strongest desire to love someone proves that there is a person with whom we are in love. All it proves is our need and perhaps our capacity. [...]

If the psychoanalyst is primarily interested in the human reality behind religious doctrines, he will find the same reality underlying different religions and opposite human attitudes underlying the same religion. The human reality, for instance, underlying the teachings of Buddha, Isaiah, Christ, Socrates, or Spinoza is essentially the same. It is determined by the striving for love, truth, and justice. The human reality behind Calvin's theological system and that of authoritarian political systems is also very similar. Their spirit is one of submission to power and lack of love and of respect for the individual.

Just as a parent's consciously felt or expressed concern for a child can be an expression of love or can express a wish for control and domination, a religious statement can be expressive of opposite human attitudes. We do not discard that statement but look at it in perspective, the human reality behind it providing the third dimension. Particularly concerning the sincerity of the postulate of love the words hold true: "By their fruits shall ye know them." If religious teachings contribute to the growth, strength, freedom, and happiness of their believers, we see the fruits of love. If they contribute to the constriction of human potentialities, to unhappiness and lack of productivity, they cannot be born of love, regardless of what the dogma intends to convey.

19

Religious Experience and the Concept of God

Is religious experience necessarily connected with a theistic concept? I believe not; one can describe a "religious" experience as a human experience which underlies, and is common to, certain types of theistic, as well as nontheistic, atheistic, or even antitheistic conceptualizations. What differs is the conceptualization of the experience, not the experiential substratum underlying various conceptualizations. This type of experience is most clearly expressed in Christian, Moslem, and Jewish mysticism, as well as in Zen Buddhism. If one analyzes the experience rather than the conceptualization, therefore, one can speak of a *theistic as well as of a nontheistic religious experience*.

There remains the epistemological difficulty. There is no word for the substratum of this type of religious experience in Western languages, except when it is referred to in connection with theism. Hence it is ambiguous to use the word *religious*; even the word *spiritual* is not much better, since it has other misleading connotations. For these reasons I think it is preferable to speak, at least in this book, of the *x experience*, which is found in religious and in philosophical systems (such as that of Spinoza), regardless of whether they do or do not have a concept of God.

A psychological analysis of the *x* experience would go far beyond the scope of this book. However, in order to indicate briefly at least some of the main aspects of the phenomenon, I suggest the following points:

1. The first characteristic element is *to experience life as a problem*, as a "question" that requires an answer. The non-*x* person does not feel a deep, or at least not a conscious, disquiet about the existential dichotomies of life. Life as such is not a problem for him; he is not bothered by the need for a solution. He is—at least consciously—satisfied with finding

the meaning of life in work or pleasure or power or fame or even, like the ethical man, in acting in accordance with his conscience. To him mundane life makes sense, and he does not experience the pain of his separateness from man and nature nor the passionate wish to overcome this separateness and to find at-one-ment.

2. For the x experience there exists a definite hierarchy of values. The highest value is the optimal development of one's own powers of reason, love, compassion, courage. All worldly achievements are subordinated to these highest human (or spiritual, or x) values. This hierarchy of values does not imply asceticism; it does not exclude worldly pleasures and joys, but it makes the worldly life part of the spiritual life; or rather, the worldly life is permeated by the spiritual aims.

3. Related to the hierarchy of values is another aspect of the x experience. For the average person, especially in a materialistic culture, life is a means toward ends other than the person himself. These ends are: pleasure, money, power, the production and distribution of commodities, and so on. If man is not used by others for their ends, he uses himself for his own; in both cases he becomes a means. For the x person, man alone is an end and never a means. Furthermore, his whole attitude toward life is one in which each event is responded to from the standpoint of whether or not it helps to transform him in the direction of becoming more human. Whether it is art or science, joy or sorrow, work or play, whatever happens is a stimulus to his becoming stronger and more sensitive. This process of constant inner transformation and of becoming part of the world in the act of living is the aim toward which all other aims are subordinated. Man is not a subject opposing the world in order to transform *it*; he is *in* the world making his being in the world the occasion for constant self-transformation. Hence the world (man and nature) is not an object standing opposite to him, but the medium in which he discovers his own reality and that of the world ever more deeply. Neither is he a "subject," the least indivisible part of human substance (an atom, an individual), not even Descartes' lofty thinking subject, but a self that is alive and strong precisely to the degree to which it ceases to hold onto itself, but *is* by responding.

4. More specifically, the x attitude can be described in the following terms: a letting go of one's "ego," one's greed, and with it, of one's fears; a giving up the wish to hold onto the "ego" as if it were an indestructible, separate entity; a making oneself empty in order to be able to fill oneself with the world, to respond to it, to become one with it, to love it. To make oneself empty does not express passivity but *openness*. Indeed, if one cannot make oneself empty, how can one respond to the world? How

can one see, hear, feel, love, if one is filled with one's ego, if one is driven by greed?

5. The x experience can also be called one of transcendence. But here again we find the same problem as in the case of the word *religious*. *Transcendence* is conventionally used in the sense of God's transcendence. But as a human phenomenon we deal with transcending the ego, leaving the prison of one's selfishness and separateness; whether we conceive of this transcendence as one toward God is a matter of conceptualization. The experience is essentially the same whether it refers to God or not.

The x experience, whether theistic or not, is characterized by the reduction, and, in its fullest form, by the disappearance, of narcissism. In order to be open to the world, to transcend my ego, I must be able to reduce or to give up my narcissism. I must, furthermore, give up all forms of incestuous fixation and of greed; I must overcome my destructiveness and necrophilous tendencies. I must be able to love life. I must also have a criterion for differentiating between a false x experience, rooted in hysteria and other forms of mental illness, and the nonpathological experience of love and union. I must have a concept of true independence, must be able to differentiate between rational and irrational authority, between idea and ideology, between willingness to suffer for my convictions and masochism.

It follows from all the foregoing considerations that the analysis of the x experience moves from the level of theology to that of psychology and, especially, psychoanalysis. First of all, because it is necessary to differentiate between conscious thought and affective experience, which may or may not be expressed in adequate conceptualizations. Secondly, because psychoanalytic theory permits an understanding of those unconscious experiences which underly the x experience or, on the other hand, those which are opposed to it or block it. Without an understanding of unconscious processes, it is difficult to appreciate the relative and often accidental character of our conscious thoughts. However, in order to understand the x experience, psychoanalysis must enlarge its conceptual frame beyond that outlined by Freud. The central problem of man is not that of his libido; it is that of dichotomies inherent in his existence, his separateness, alienation, suffering, his fear of freedom, his wish for union, his capacity for hate and destruction, his capacity for love and union.

In short, we are in need of an empirical psychological anthropology which studies x and non-x experience as experiential human phenomena, regardless of conceptualizations. Such a study might lead to establishing rationally the superiority of the x way to all others, as methodologically the Buddha already did. It may occur that while the Middle Ages were concerned with the proof of God's existence with philosophical and logical arguments, the future will be concerned with outlining the essential rightness of the x way on the basis of a highly developed anthropology. [. . .]

The idea of the one God expresses a new answer for the solution of the dichotomies of human existence; man can find oneness with the world, not by regressing to the prehuman state, but by the full development of his specifically human qualities: love and reason. The worship of God is first of all the negation of idolatry. The concept of God is at first formed according to the political and social concepts of a tribal chief or king. The image is then developed of a constitutional monarch who is obligated to man to abide by his own principles: love and justice. He becomes the nameless God, the God about whom no attribute of essence can be predicated. This God without attributes, who is worshiped "in silence," has ceased to be an authoritarian God; man must become fully independent, and that means independent even from God. In "negative theology," as well as in mysticism, we find the same revolutionary spirit of freedom which characterized the God of the revolution against Egypt. I could not express this spirit better than by quoting Meister Eckhart:

> That I am a man
> I have in common with all men,
> That I see and hear
> And eat and drink
> I share with all animals.
> But that I am I is exclusively mine,
> And belongs to me
> And to nobody else,
> To no other man
> Nor to an angel nor to God,
> Except inasmuch as I am one with him.

Fragments (My translation—E. F.)

20

De-Repression and Enlightenment: Psychoanalysis and Zen Buddhism

The aim of Zen is enlightenment: the immediate, unreflected grasp of reality, without affective contamination and intellectualization, the realization of the relation of myself to the universe. This new experience is a repetition of the preintellectual, immediate grasp of the child, but on a new level, that of the full development of man's reason, objectivity, individuality. While the child's experience, that of immediacy and oneness, lies *before* the experience of alienation and the subject-object split, the enlightenment experience lies after it.

The aim of psychoanalysis, as formulated by Freud, is that of making the unconscious conscious, of replacing id by ego. To be sure, the content of the unconscious to be discovered was limited to a small sector of the personality, to those instinctual drives which were alive in early childhood, but which were subject to amnesia. To lift these out of the state of repression was the aim of the analytic technique. Furthermore, the sector to be uncovered, quite aside from Freud's theoretical premises, was determined by the therapeutic need to cure a particular symptom. There was little interest in recovering unconsciousness outside of the sector related to the symptom formation. Slowly the introduction of the concept of the death instinct and Eros and the development of the ego aspects in recent years have brought about a certain broadening of the Freudian concepts of the contents of the unconscious. The non-Freudian schools greatly widened the sector of the unconscious to be uncovered. Most radically Jung, but also Adler, Rank, and the other more recent so-called neo-Freudian authors have contributed to this extension. But (with the exception of Jung), in spite of such a widening, the extent of the sector to be uncovered has remained determined by the therapeutic aim of curing this or that symptom; or this or that neurotic character trait. It has not encompassed the whole person.

However, if one follows the original aim of Freud, that of making the unconscious conscious, to its last consequences, one must free it from the limitations imposed on it by Freud's own instinctual orientation, and by the immediate task of curing symptoms. If one pursues the aim of the full recovery of the unconscious, then this task is not restricted to the instincts, nor to other limited sectors of experience, but to the total experience of the total man; then the aim becomes that of overcoming alienation, and of the subject-object split in perceiving the world; then the uncovering of the unconscious means the overcoming of affective contamination and cerebration; it means the de-repression, the abolition of the split within myself between the universal man and the social man; it means the disappearance of the polarity of conscious versus unconscious; it means arriving at the state of the immediate grasp of reality, without distortion and without interference by intellectual reflection; it means overcoming of the craving to hold on to the ego, to worship it; it means giving up the illusion of an indestructible separate ego, which is to be enlarged, preserved and as the Egyptian pharaohs hoped to preserve themselves as mummies for eternity. To be conscious of the unconscious means to be open, responding, to *have* nothing and to *be*.

This aim of the full recovery of unconsciousness by consciousness is quite obviously much more radical than the general psychoanalytic aim. The reasons for this are easy to see. To achieve this total aim requires an effort far beyond the effort most persons in the West are willing to make. But quite aside from this question of effort, even the visualization of this aim is possible only under certain conditions. First of all, this radical aim can be envisaged only from the point of view of a certain philosophical position. There is no need to describe this position in detail. Suffice it to say that it is one in which not the negative aim of the absence of sickness, but the positive one of the presence of well-being is aimed at, and that well-being is conceived in terms of full union, the immediate and uncontaminated grasp of the world. This aim could not be better described than has been done by Suzuki in terms of "the art of living." One must keep in mind that any such concept as the art of living grows from the soil of a spiritual humanistic orientation, as it underlies the teaching of Buddha, of the prophets, of Jesus, of Meister Eckhart, or of men such as Blake, Walt Whitman, or Bucke. Unless it is seen in this context, the concept of "the art of living" loses all that is specific, and deteriorates into a concept that goes today under the name of "happiness." It must also not be forgotten that this orientation includes an ethical aim. While Zen transcends ethics, it includes the basic ethical aims of Buddhism, which are essentially the same as those of all humanistic teaching. The achievement of the aim of Zen, as Suzuki has made very clear, implies the overcoming of greed in all forms, whether it is the greed for possession, for fame, or for affection; it implies overcoming narcissistic self-glorification and the illusion of omnipotence. It implies, furthermore, the overcoming of the desire to submit to an authority who solves one's own problem of existence. The person who only wants to use the discovery of the unconscious to be cured of sickness will, of course, not even attempt to achieve the radical aim which lies in the overcoming of repressedness.

But it would be a mistake to believe that the radical aim of the de-repression has no connection with a therapeutic aim. Just as one has recognized that the cure of a symptom and the prevention of future symptom formations are not possible without the analysis and change of the character, one must also recognize that the change of this or that neurotic character trait is not possible without pursuing the more radical aim of a complete transformation of the person. It may very well be that the relatively disappointing results of character analysis (which have never been expressed more honestly than by Freud in his "Analysis, Terminable or Interminable?") are due precisely to the fact that the aims for the cure of the neurotic character were not radical enough; that well-being, freedom from anxiety and insecurity, can be achieved only if the limited aim is transcended, that is, if one realizes that the limited, therapeutic aim cannot be achieved as long as it remains limited and does not become part of a wider, humanistic frame of reference. Perhaps the limited aim can be achieved with more limited and less time-consuming methods, while the time and energy consumed in the long analytic process are used fruitfully only for the radical aim of "transformation" rather than the narrow one of "reform." [. . .] Man, as long as he has not reached the creative relatedness of which *satori* is the fullest achievement, at best compensates for inherent potential depression by routine, idolatry, destructiveness, greed for property or fame, etc. When any of these compensations break down, his sanity is threatened. The cure of the potential insanity lies only in the change in attitude from split and alienation to the creative, immediate grasp of and response to the world. If psychoanalysis can help in this way, it can help to achieve true mental health; if it cannot, it will only help to improve compensatory mechanisms. To put it still differently: Somebody may be "cured" of a symptom, but he cannot be "cured" of a character neurosis. Man is not a thing, man is not a "case," and the analyst does not cure anybody by treating him as an object. Rather, the analyst can only help a man to wake up, in a process in which the analyst is engaged with the "patient" in the process of their understanding each other, which means experiencing their oneness.

In stating all this, however, we must be prepared to be confronted with an objection. If, as I said above, the achievement of the full consciousness of the unconscious is as radical and difficult an aim as enlightenment, does it make any sense to discuss this radical aim as something which has any general application? Is it not purely speculative to raise seriously the question that only this radical aim can justify the hopes of psychoanalytic therapy?

If there were only the alternative between full enlightenment and nothing, then indeed this objection would be valid. But this is not so. In Zen there are many stages of enlightenment, of which *satori* is the ultimate and decisive step. But, as far as I understand, value is set on experiences, which are steps in the direction of *satori*, although *satori* may never be reached. Dr. Suzuki once illustrated this point in the following way: If one candle is brought into an absolutely dark room, the darkness disappears, and there is light. But if ten or a hundred or a thousand candles are added, the room will become brighter and brighter. Yet the decisive change was brought about by the first candle which penetrated the darkness.

What happens in the analytic process? A person senses for the first time that he is vain, that he is frightened, that he hates, while consciously he had believed himself to be modest, brave, and loving. The new insight may hurt him, but it opens a door; it permits him to stop projecting on others what he represses in himself. He proceeds; he experiences the infant, the child, the adolescent, the criminal, the insane, the saint, the artist, the male, *and* the female within himself; he gets more deeply in touch with humanity, with the universal man; he represses less, is freer, has less need to project, to cerebrate; then he may experience for the first time how he sees colors, how he sees a ball roll, how his ears are suddenly fully opened to music, when up to now he only listened *to* it; in sensing his oneness with others, he may have a first glimpse of the illusion that his separate individual ego is some*thing* to hold onto, to cultivate, to save; he will experience the futility of seeking the answer to life by *having* himself, rather than by being and becoming himself. All these are sudden, unexpected experiences with no intellectual content; yet afterwards the person feels freer, stronger, less anxious than he ever felt before.

So far we have spoken about *aims*, and I have proposed that if one carries Freud's principle of the transformation of unconsciousness into consciousness to its ultimate consequences, one approaches the concept of enlightenment. But as to *methods* of achieving this aim, psychoanalysis and Zen are, indeed, entirely different. The method of Zen is, one might say, that of a frontal attack on the alienated way of perception by means of the "sitting," the koan, and the authority of the master. Of course, all this is not a "technique" which can be isolated from the premise of Buddhist thinking, of the behavior and ethical values which are embodied in the master and in the atmosphere of the monastery. It must also be remembered that it is not a "five hour a week" concern, and that by the very fact of coming for instruction in Zen the student has made a most important decision, a decision which is an important part of what goes on afterwards.

The psychoanalytic method is entirely different from the Zen method. It trains consciousness to get hold of the unconscious in a different way. It directs attention to that perception which is distorted; it leads to a recognition of the fiction within oneself; it widens the range of human experience by lifting repressedness. The analytic method is psychological-empirical. It examines the psychic development of a person from childhood on and tries to recover earlier experiences in order to assist the person in experiencing of what is now repressed. It proceeds by uncovering illusions within oneself about the world, step by step, so that paratactic distortions and alienated intellectualizations diminish. By becoming less of a stranger to himself, the person who goes through this process becomes less estranged to the world; because he has opened up communication with the universe within himself, he has opened up communication with the universe outside. False consciousness disappears, and with it the polarity conscious-unconscious. A new realism dawns in which "the mountains are mountains again." The psychoanalytic method is of course only a method, a preparation; but so is the Zen method. By the very fact that it is a method it never guarantees the achievement of the goal. The factors which permit this achievement are deeply rooted in the individual personality, and for all practical purposes we know little of them.

I have suggested that the method of uncovering the unconscious, if carried to its ultimate consequences, may be a step toward enlightenment, provided it is taken within the philosophical context which is most radically and realistically expressed in Zen. But only a great deal of further experience in applying this method will show how far it can lead. The view expressed here implies only a possibility and thus has the character of a hypothesis which is to be tested.

But what can be said with more certainty is that the knowledge of Zen, and a concern with it, can have a most fertile and clarifying influence on the theory and technique of psychoanalysis. Zen, different as it is in its method from psychoanalysis, can sharpen the focus, throw new light on the nature of insight, and heighten the sense of what it is to see, what it is to be creative, what it is to overcome the affective contaminations and false intellectualizations which are the necessary results of experience based on the subject-object split.

In its very radicalism with respect to intellectualization, authority, and the delusion of the ego, in its emphasis on the aim of well-being, Zen thought will deepen and widen the horizon of the psychoanalyst and help him to arrive at a more radical concept of the grasp of reality as the ultimate aim of full, conscious awareness.

If further speculation on the relation between Zen and psychoanalysis is permissible, one might think of the possibility that psychoanalysis may be significant to the student of Zen. I can visualize it as a help in avoiding the danger of a false enlightenment (which is, of course, no enlightenment), one which is purely subjective, based on psychotic or hysterical phenomena, or on a self-induced state of trance. Analytic clarification might help the Zen student to avoid illusions, the absence of which is the very condition of enlightenment.

Whatever the use is that Zen may make of psychoanalysis, from the standpoint of a Western psychoanalyst I express my gratitude for this precious gift of the East, especially to Dr. Suzuki, who has succeeded in expressing it in such a way that none of its essence becomes lost in the attempt to translate Eastern into Western thinking, so that the Westerner, if he takes the trouble, can arrive at an understanding of Zen, as far as it can be arrived at before the goal is reached. How could such understanding be possible, were it not for the fact that "Buddha nature is in all of us," that man and existence are universal categories, and that the immediate grasp of reality, waking up, and enlightenment, are universal experiences.

Index